NEW WRITING / BOOK TALK / NE

THE REA

No. 68 WINTER 2017-18

Published by The Reader

The
Reader

CONNECT
REALISE
CHANGE

EDITOR   Philip Davis

DEPUTY EDITOR   Sarah Coley
CO-EDITORS   Marjorie Lotfi Gill
                                Angela Macmillan
                                Fiona Magee
                                Brian Nellist

ADDRESS   The Reader Magazine,
                                The Reader,
                                Calderstones Mansion House,
                                Calderstones Park,
                                Liverpool,
                                L18 3JB

EMAIL   magazine@thereader.org.uk
WEBSITE   www.thereader.org.uk

DISTRIBUTION   See p. 127

COVER   Artwork by Nigel Luckhurst

ISBN 978-0-9935610-7-8

SUBMISSIONS

The Reader genuinely welcomes submissions of previously unpublished poetry, fiction, essays, readings and thought. We publish professional writers and absolute beginners. Send your manuscript with SAE please to:

The Reader, Magazine Submissions, Calderstones Mansion House, Calderstones Park, Liverpool, L18 3JB

Printed and bound in the European Union by Bell and Bain Ltd, Glasgow

THE READER MANIFESTO

The Reader is a literary magazine that does not believe in literature just for literature's sake: it believes that literature is useful to human beings. Useful, but not in terms of a world of cold calculation, set opinion or reductive summary. For us reading is more than that: more than information-processing, more also than entertainment or escapism, more than the academic or specialist: it is the best way of thinking deeply, emotionally, personally and subtly about existence. We want to do work, to-and-fro, in the middle ground *between* literature and life.

The Reader, as a magazine, is an arm of The Reader charity, and shares its mission of bringing about a Reading Revolution. Where the charity develops and supports Shared Reading groups, including in its communities those people who might not normally think of themselves as readers, the magazine tries to reach individuals who may already be serious readers, wherever they may be found, and seeks to bring them together through the printed page. And on its pages, in the effort to break down fixed demarcations, it also brings together:

- New Writing and the continuing power of Old Poems and Past Fictions
- Non-fictional stories and interviews that put Lives alongside Books
- The most Challenging Thoughts with the most Practical Suggestions.

Join us.

The Reader

CONNECT
REALISE
CHANGE

CONTENTS

The Printed Voice of The Reader

THOUGHT

BOOKSHELF

THE READER ROOM

RECOMMENDATIONS

NEWS AND EVENTS

To keep up-to-date with the latest Reader news and events sign up to our bi-monthly email newsletters at thereader.org.uk.

Friend of the Reader

Become a Reader Friend and be part of something very special. In 2018, our patron, Frank Cottrell Boyce will create a bespoke story for The Reader which will draw on personal contributions from our Reader Friends – your story will become part of ours. Become a Reader Friend and you'll also receive a welcome pack, offers and invitations to special events at our HQ in Calderstones Park: www.thereader.org.uk/support/friends/

Major new investment

We're delighted to announce a major investment from the Steve Morgan Foundation which will support our families programme and significantly improve the life chances of children living across the North West. Working with a range of partners across the region, The Reader will create engaging and enjoyable opportunities for children and families to build positive and rewarding relationships with books and reading. Find out more:www.thereader.org.uk/news/archive/

The Big Give's Christmas Challenge 2017

The Reader would like to extend a huge thank you to all our supporters who donated to our Big Give Christmas Challenge 2017. Your support helped to raise over £45,000 which will recruit, train and support volunteer Reader Leaders to bring weekly Shared Reading groups to socially isolated older people in care homes and community settings across the UK. Read more: www.blog.thereader.org.uk/christmaschallengeroundup

EDITORIAL

'MICHAEL FINNEGAN'

Philip Davis

I n Doris Lessing's *Shikasta* an emissary from another planet travels to what is a version of our earth to warn its inhabitants that they are about to undergo – are already undergoing – a period of terrible degeneration as a result of a cosmic disaster. They will become mentally lesser beings. But they cannot take it in. It is partly to do with resistance but more to do with the loss in intelligence that has already taken place. Writes the emissary, Johor, his head whirling with a sense of paradox: 'These poor creatures already did not know what had been lost.' If they had fully known it, had fully appreciated the significance of their inner deterioration, they would not have already lost it. It is like giving an already declining patient a diagnosis of dementia, where the doctor alone knows just how bad this is going to be. Johor turns to David, one of the still brightest among them, but what is the point of warning him? Dear Reader: would *you*?

> Why was I saying that? and that? his troubled eyes asked of my face: What did I mean? His questions at such moments were as if I had never taught him anything at all. He was like one drugged or in shock… It was as if a part of him knew and remembered all I told him, but other parts had not heard a word! I have never before

or since had so strongly that experience of being with a person and knowing that all the time there was certainly a part of that person in contact with you, something real and alive and listening – yet most of the time what one said did not reach that silent and invisible being, and what *he* said was not often said by the real part of him.

When I first read this, in 1982, it made me think about what was Intelligence. Here it means the capacity to think, to realise, even when the thought threatens to diagnose and overwhelm the very mind that thinks it. It is a form of Life, of greater animation, now increasingly to be lost in the dulling of a doomed planet.

I hadn't thought of Intelligence like that before. In universities, where I have worked, there are plenty of clever people. And rightly or wrongly, it was often a Cleverness that I had little time for. It seemed a secondary quality, a cover often provided by a wide vocabulary in order to be able to talk *about* things. Which was often a way of not being *in* them. 'What he said was not often said by the real part of him.' For the Clever – rather than the shocked or damaged as David is – the responses come too easily, too articulately, and take their origin from somewhere too far up in the creature, without emotional cost.

On the other hand, I recently found this from a poet I knew a little, who died in 2000 at the age of 62. He was Douglas Oliver, writing in a letter to a fellow-poet at the very end of 1970:

> I come down to this fact: there is in me – and I swear in most other people too – an area which is basically stupid, quite unargued, perhaps nineteenth century, perhaps suburban, whatever. It is an area I can easily ignore, for which I have many available antidotes (sometimes they are masks); but ultimately I cannot escape it because its foundation is the necessary impossibility of knowing fully all that we 'know'. You take the current English or American poet. You know damn well that stupidity is there but it never appears in a text that is, in every one of its stages, clever.

I will put this too starkly. But Douglas Oliver existed formidably between two worlds – that of his extraordinarily intelligent one-time mentor in Cambridge, J.H. Prynne, and that of his innocent son, whom he lost early, with Down's syndrome.

My friend Wil Sanders died in 2002, aged 65. In this issue I reprint, with the permission of his wife Jenny, an essay distilled from some of the lectures he gave in the 70s which were reprinted in the now defunct *New Universities Quarterly*. It is a voice I miss, not least because Will never tried to be clever. Sometimes it meant he reacted too quickly in dismissal of thoughts and ideas that did not seem immediately to his purpose, though he was also good at changing his mind. When we first met in Cambridge, he had been designated as my Ph.D supervisor and neither of us seemed very happy about that. We needed some raw skirmishes, also a few drinks, to get over the initial obstacles. One of the best early moments was intelligent. At the time, I remember, I had a nervous habit of saying, 'Are you sure?' when someone made me some offer or proffered some kindness. It must have been annoying. All Wil said to me was that I shouldn't do that secondary thing; I should take what I wanted the first time round. And the frank, untroubled tone in which he said it allowed me to take it in. Some of that freedom is, I think, in that essay. Of which he said to me, during one of his lower times, I wish I could remember who wrote that.

But I best got to know him by reading him. It may sound ironic or academic or secondary but really it wasn't. He gave me the manuscript of a long novel he had been writing. It was called 'Poor Old Michael Finnigan' from the verse for children:

> There was an old man named Michael Finnegan
> He grew fat and then grew thin again
> Then he died and had to begin again
> Poor old Michael Finnegan
> Begin again.

It was the story of a man whose eldest child had died, and the attempts somehow to begin again a life at first hand. It was a big, messy, hearted and generous novel, full of intelligence, full of stupidity. And it was never published.

It was a terrible waste, an injustice rationalised by clever publishing firms. But, for all his exuberant determination, I don't think Wil ever quite recovered from the loss of that book in failing to redeem other losses. I used to visit Wil and Jenny in that large living room of theirs in the house they occupied in Grange Road next to Selwyn College. And there on the wall was Jenny's large painting of Claire, the daughter they had both, each, lost in a road accident. It made me feel happy, and it is reproduced as the cover of this issue.

Writing that last sentence, I remembered something from the first line of a poem, or saw I was remembering it. Wil loved the poetry of Ben Jonson, from the strong tradition within sixteenth and seventeenth-century English verse, though Wil was resistant to religion and false comforts. 'On My First Daughter', named Mary – this is the verse:

> Here lies, to each her parents' ruth,
> Mary, the daughter of their youth;
> Yet all heaven's gifts being heaven's due,
> It makes the father less to rue.
> At six months' end she parted hence
> With safety of her innocence;
> Whose soul heaven's queen, whose name she bears,
> In comfort of her mother's tears,
> Hath placed amongst her virgin-train:
> Where, while that severed doth remain,
> This grave partakes the fleshly birth;
> Which cover lightly, gentle earth!

It was the word 'each', not merely both, in line 1; or 'their youth' now ruined, in line 2; or only 'less' not 'not', in line 4; and 'her mother' in 8 gently related to 'the father', Jonson himself, bereft in 4. 'With safety', 'In comfort', 'amongst' and so on – these are the small restrained achievements. But it is the last line of course that quietly says good night.

THOUGHT!

('A Bear of Very Little Brain')

A. A. MILNE

WHEN WE WERE VERY YOUNG

Frank Cottrell Boyce

f I didn't believe in the power of having some poetry off by heart, I would have been converted one day about ten years ago when we were stuck in a horrendous, endless, meaningless traffic jam. My daughter – then aged about four – suddenly piped up and recited the whole of Julia Donaldson's *The Gruffalo*. None of us had any idea she'd learnt it. It lit up the day. Years later I was interviewing men who had been prisoners of the Japanese on the Burma railway. A surprising number of them talked about how being able to recite gave them – and their listeners – a moment of respite. A.A. Milne had an incomparable gift for making poems with surprising rhymes and lovely, lithe rhythms that touch and transform the real feelings of childhood into spectacle and fairy tale. I love 'The King's Breakfast'. It has the rhythm of a skipping game but it's really an account of a typical toddler tantrum transformed into a kind of pantomime by swopping the toddler for a king.

The King sobbed, 'Oh, deary me!'
And went back to bed.
'Nobody,'
He whimpered,
'Could call me
A fussy man;
I only want
A little bit
Of butter for
My bread!'

This is the book in which Winnie the Pooh makes his very first appearance. It's in the poem 'Teddy Bear' which tells the story of how a 'short and fat' bear who is worried about his weight becomes reconciled to his own appearance when he bumps into the equally chubby King of France.

Our Teddy answered not a word;
It's doubtful if he even heard.
Our bear could only look and look:
The stout man in the picture-book!
That 'handsome' King – could this be he,
This man of adiposity?

It's not by any means the best poem in the book and there's nothing to suggest that the bear in the poem will within a couple of years be a global phenomenon that will make his author wealthy and unhappy. Although it's always struck me as a bit ominous that the bear in the illustration for the poem is wearing a shirt – as the Disney Winnie will do but as Shepherd's Winnie never did again.

Christopher Robin also makes his debut here in 'Vespers – Little Boy Kneels at the Foot of the Bed'. The poem was an instant success when it was first published in *Vanity Fair* and it was this that gave Milne the motivation to go on and write more about the boy, which was a catastrophically bad parenting decision but a great creative one. One of the other poems in here – 'Buckingham Palace' – comes in for a good kicking in Christopher Robin's memoir *The Enchanted Places* because the Nanny in the poem is dismissive of the boy's questions.

They're changing guard at Buckingham Palace –
Christopher Robin went down with Alice.
'Do you think the King knows all about me?'
'Sure to, dear, but it's time for tea,'
Says Alice.

Christopher Robin said his real nanny – Olive Rand – would never have acted like that. Money, family ruptures, bad parenting – the book has dark roots and darker fruits. But Milne's extraordinary virtuosity gives it a lovely, breezy carelessness, like a stick being twirled by a child on a Summer walk. The poem 'Disobedience' for instance deals with the most intense and primal childhood fear – the loss of your mother – but it tames that fear by dazzling it with the games it plays with words and letters and even typography. It's plucked from Milne's heart and it cries out to be learned by your heart.

James James
Morrison's mother
Hasn't been heard of since.
King John said he was sorry,
So did the Queen and Prince.
King John
(Somebody told me)
Said to a man he knew:
'If people go down to the end of the town, well,
what can anyone do?'

The new film *Goodbye Christopher Robin* is written by Frank Cottrell Boyce from a story by Simon Vaughn.

POETRY

RICHARD MEIER

The answer

Where in the whole world would you like to be right now?
a girl I once liked asked me. Meaning me to say
the Hindu Kush, I think, or *Angkor Wat*,
not *It depends on who was there.*
Asked now, I'd answer

Norfolk – and mean
its northeasternmost scrap we've often
bolted to, mean its dunes, a sheet of paper torn
lengthways, then turned landscape; and here and there,
the pinnacled church towers, like long-eared owls, and you.

The tree

Gingko, declares my mother,
sat at the table thumbing,
or leafing rather, through
the tree book to discover
whose leaf it is Matilda
has brought home from the park.

And, bingo, there it is –
the self-same, ribbed, fan-shape.
And she must think, my daughter,
this process simple, common –
the seeing, then recognition,
of things and so of people.

Restoration project

Small bedroom chair (Edwardian?),
curved cane seat stove in,
as if punched, once, hard.

More likely this harm stems
from someone reaching, someone
who – all their focus on

the wanted thing – forgot,
if they had ever known,
the nature of that which bore,

even lifted them.

Last chance

What are you doing, Daddy? asks the boy
discovering his father in the long, west-facing garden.
Just sitting in the sun, he answers, sketchily –

it's too soon for his three year-old to face
I'm savouring the last bit of the light, and so on.
What are you doing now? the boy asks sometime later,

the sun-patch less an oblong than a square,
though soon, in truth, rectangular again,
but crossways now, a slab across the garden.

And when the boy returns he calls out
Why are you standing there against the wall, Daddy?
Why are you standing on that chair?

ESSAY

WHO OWNS LITERATURE?

Wilbur Sanders

The proverbial wisdom has it that people who live in glass houses shouldn't throw stones. It depends how you feel about living in a glasshouse really. They can be stuffy places, filled with a great deal of forced vegetation, so airless at times that the risk of a few flying splinters seems negligible beside the relief a fresh breeze would bring. And perhaps the most exasperating thing about the literary glasshouse is that, if you raise your eyes, you can see the great world out there, full of inviting vistas – indeed you spend your time, eyes down, reading all about it.

It's arguable, of course, that any sensible person suffering from this claustrophobia won't start pitching bricks. He'll walk out through the door. My experience of attempting this simple exit, however, has frequently brought me nose to nose with some extremely sour-visaged academic heavies who have posted themselves at the door. The guardians of the glasshouse protocol: 'Plac'd at the door of learning, youth to guide,/We never suffer it to stand too wide'.

They take many shapes, these guardians: all crying with one voice, 'You can't say that! Not in *our* greenhouse!'

Well, I'm sorry, but I'm going to. Going to say things harmless and ridiculous, though I hope salutary. Things that the world well knows, yet none knows well. For a start…

Truism 1. *The writing of books is not the supreme human activity.* The quality of human life is more important than what is said about it, and the justification of literature must lie, if anywhere, in the way it serves that life, not in its own self-enclosed activity. It's the mark of a great writer, often, to see this very starkly; he often has spells of going right off literature for exactly that reason. 'Life is short', Tolstoy wrote to an importunate publisher in 1859, 'and to waste it in my adult years writing… stories… makes me feel ashamed. I can and must and want to get down to business' (*Letters*, I, 129). Critics with a heavy investment in the literary commodities market want to laugh this off: it's a temporary aberration, a venial insincerity, a momentary coyness. It's not. It's the mainspring of Tolstoy's greatness that he doesn't care about literature. Only by not caring about it was he freed to put into literature the life-content that made it worth caring about.

Fitting *things to words*, Wordsworth once wrote, was no more than 'a juggler's trick'. The 'noble employment' was 'fitting words to things' – and in the things thus represented lay writing's justification ('Essay on Morals'). Critics, again, will try to whittle this intransigence away as an over-simplification of the relation between words and things. Maybe it is. But it is nevertheless Wordsworth's final and non-negotiable position.

Truism 2. *Criticism is unnecessary.* Not the self-criticism of the author (which is an integral part of the writing), but the vast body of reviews, monographs, scholarly articles &c. One of the ages that produced least criticism (and that of the poorest) was the Elizabethan/Jacobean age. And no period has been so stupefyingly prolific of criticism as our own. Is the correlation manifest? Isn't it the mark of the greatest works to be so complete in their own terms that we feel a kind of helplessness in attempting to add anything of our own? Certainly all the works I most admire leave me with a happy conviction that there's no need for me or anyone else to say a damn thing. It's all there. It's been done.

It's natural that professionals will try to justify their own activities; modestly insinuate that the critic, like the humble earthworm, performs a more important function in the estate of letters than his lowliness might suggest; or hint that criticism, at its best, is a kind of literature. But I suggest that a genuine criticism is more likely to result from recognising that the work doesn't need us. And as for that last suggestion – that criticism can be a kind of literature – let me just note that if it *does* achieve that emancipation, it will no longer be referring itself to the literature for justification. The relation will not be one of servant to master, but of brother to brother. The best criticism often does strike a significantly *fraternal* note. And it is usually written by someone who has some independent claim on the title of writer.

But literature doesn't *need* criticism. It just (human nature being what it is) gets it, and probably always will. It's a wholly natural activity – arguing and disputing about books. Can be highly pleasurable. And I'm not complaining. But do let's stop pretending we do it for the author's sake.

Truism 3. *No major author writes* (though some minor ones may) *to be read primarily by critics or scholars.* Literature was not designed for those who regard themselves as its principal and most discerning consumers. Indeed there is an ancient and deep-rooted animosity between authors and critics – usually with the authors complaining that the critics, in their vanity of censure, simply cannot read:

> The whole set of 'em [rages Tristram Shandy] are so hung round and befetished with the bobs and trinkets of criticism... their heads, Sir, are so stuck full of rules and compasses, and have that eternal propensity to apply them on all occasions, that a work of genius had better go to the devil at once, than stand to be pricked and tortured to death by 'em... Grant me patience, just Heaven! – Of all the cants which are canted in this canting world – though the cant of hypocrites may be the worst – the cant of criticism is the most tormenting!
>
> I would go fifty miles on foot, for I have not a horse worth riding on, to kiss the hand of that man whose generous heart will give up the reins of his imagination into his author's hands – be pleased he knows not why, and cares not wherefore.
>
> (Laurence Sterne, *Tristram Shandy*, III, xii)

Sterne, in his forthright fashion, declares war. What the critic sees as his unique equipment for the task is for the author the mark of his disqualification. Rules and compasses. Sterne appeals out and away from the professional critic, to that more generous reader who is capable of giving up the reins of his or her imagination.

The researcher, or critic, who understands this has one prime task: he must deconstruct himself as expert, and reconstitute himself as reader. He must, as it were, rejoin the rest of humanity before he can even hear what is being said. You learn in order to be able creatively to forget. We are all 'common readers'. The only uncommon thing, in the halls of learning, is to be aware of the fact.

Truism 4. *Literature is not something concerning which you can ascertain the truth…* since it's not only endlessly manifold in itself, but it involves a further (highly various) variable – the reader. When a friend of Tolstoy's wrote offering an interpretation of *Anna Karenina*, and inquiring whether he'd understood the novel correctly, Tolstoy was nonplussed. 'It's *one* of the truths which can be expressed,' he hedged. 'Your opinion is true, but it isn't everything – i.e. everything is true.' Then, feeling perhaps that this was less than lucid, he went on:

> I have been guided by the need to gather together ideas which for the purposes of self-expression were interconnected; but every idea expressed separately in words loses its meaning and is terribly impoverished when taken by itself out of the connection in which it occurs. The connection itself is made up… not by the idea, but by something else, and it is impossible to express the basis of this connection directly in words. It can only be expressed indirectly – by words describing characters, actions and situations. (*Letters*, I, 296)

Anyone can come up with an explanatory 'idea' – they're tuppence a dozen – one of the thousands of 'truths' the book might be said to embody. But it's the connectedness that counts.

The authoritative and precise and final statement is the one the author made; everything else distorts, diminishes or perverts it. 'If I were to try and say in words everything I intended to express in my novel,' (this was Tolstoy's final offer) 'I would have to write the same novel I wrote, from the beginning.'

Truism 5. The claim that one *ought* to know about this or that (the master-concepts behind all syllabuses and curricula, however liberal) is meaningless outside the coercive frame. The obligation to read is as non-existent as the right to educate. What can 'ought' mean, as applied to the processes of human assimilation? Half the time it's simply the educator's will-to-domination operating on our propensity for guilt.

One of D. H. Lawrence's friends had been assailed by one of these pedagogic dieticians, and he gave her this sound advice (Letter of 25 June 1908):

> Don't let that little fool shove a lot of mental rubbish on you. Systematic reading be damned!... If you feel like going for something wildly emotional, you have it, and don't let that pragmatical ass shove shredded what down you, when you want the red apple of feeling.

Anyway, as Dr Johnson often pointed out, systematic reading doesn't even make practical sense:

> What we read with inclination makes a much stronger impression. If we read without inclination, half the mind is employed in fixing the attention; so there is but one half to be employed on what we read. (Boswell, 12 April, 1776)

And he was equally crisp with the parallel superstition that you've got to *read everything through*. Believing, as he did, that most books contained only one thing worth knowing, he was usually content to 'look into' a book. And when someone reproached him for censuring a book he had not read through, he remarked tartly:

> Sir, when I take up the end of a web, and find it pack thread, I do not expect, by looking further, to find embroidery. (Boswell, 16 Oct, 1769)

There is, indeed, no end to the things we 'ought to know about.' But there are many ways of knowing – and being able to tell pack-thread from embroidery at a glance, is one of them.

It isn't knowledge, anyway, that results from submission

to pedagogic directives – it's neurosis. Once you allow pre-eminence to the vast number of things you *aren't* reading, you're quite incapable of attending to those you *are*; and you justify your unseemly scramble through Item A on your reading list by reference to the wild rush still to be completed through Items B – Z. Neurotic reading of this kind leaves no residue, except a collection of rattling *names*. And you can recognise those who've done a lot of it, by the way they're forever dropping them.

One needs to slow down and be patient. The day will come when an unperceived need, a vague curiosity or a felt deficiency comes to maturity and the *ought* becomes a very definite *want*. Then there is an obligation to read – an obligation you owe to yourself. The propounders of 'oughts', listened to in a spirit of dispassionate inquiry, can sometimes assist this ripening. But until that day comes the only obligation is to stop reading the moment the free intercourse of free minds becomes a coercive tedium; an obligation to keep your reserves of energy and response unimpaired for the books that really do speak to you.

What it comes down to is that we need to have the courage of our own ignorance. Ignorance is not a blank. It's a positive act – choosing not-to-read something. The peculiar personal contours of our ignorance are something we have chosen as surely as we've chosen what we shall know – it's one and the same choice. Educators ought to be sure they know what they're doing before they tamper with natural ignorance – and the implicit recommendation to students of an omniscience the recommender knows to be delusive (I'm thinking of that standard implement of educational repression – the reading list) is just such a tampering. Knowledge is the free assimilation, into the substance of my experience, of someone else's experience. It involves not-knowing as well as knowing. Also not wanting to know. And, like all life-processes, it's a long slow affair. There's a limit to what we can take in, all at once. Push too hastily beyond that limit and you'll breed monsters. I'm sure you've met them – people who've read ten times as much as they can assimilate, and are so abundantly supplied with concepts for every experience they could ever undergo, that nothing can ever happen to them – except perhaps that ghostly and disembodied experience of 'rising up the academic ladder.'

The Good Cause of which I've appointed myself spokesman, then, is the cause of the Common Reader. And the enemy is the pedagogic elite who in our age (and for the first time in history) have claimed proprietorial rights over literature. Whatever their methodological complexion (and they come in all colours and shapes), they are, I suggest, interlopers, trespassers and usurpers upon the common freehold of thinking and articulate humanity. And they must be seen off.

Another reading public has persisted unimpaired from Victorian times, taking no note of the edicts of the academies as to how it shall and shan't read – indeed, rather amused by their presumptions. People do read, outside a University, it is sometimes necessary to insist; and even inside, there's a remarkable amount of variety surviving.

And one does, of course, meet real readers in all sorts of unexpected corners – people who unmistakably *possess* the books they talk about – a 'possession' which arrogates to itself no right of disposal, only an inalienable and total right of access. Almost anyone who has cared for reading knows the feeling: certain books, certain authors are ours; we've made them our own (often by the most anarchic and haphazard process – but ours, nevertheless, we feel them to be). We may be informed by our betters that we're guilty of drastic misinterpretation. It makes no difference. We discover later that our betters were right. Still the book holds us. We turn brusque, rude, voluble. But that's all right. The critic who can talk with impeccable rationality about a work has never cared for it enough to be a good critic of it. It's right that we should feel works in this irrational, inchoate way – it shows we aren't simply submitting them to our mental predilections, shows that there is something bigger here than any of the immediate uses we may have for it. And discussion is always livelier, more vigorous and more penetrating when someone will admit himself touched and implicated, and will consent to talk boldly out of that obscure region of the mind where conviction is scarcely to be distinguished from prejudice.

Can we really hand literature over to such guardians?

It's a bit late to be worrying about that. It's already in such hands, and always has been. Unless you're prepared to instigate a licensing system by which no untrained person is allowed to open a book, there's not a lot you can do about it.

But, anyway, does it really matter, is anything seriously endangered when a work of literature is misinterpreted, even perverted? Suppose your old friend Smith has been watching, let's say, Garbo being *Anna Karenina* on the telly; and he comes up with the proposition that the film has 'really caught the spirit of the book.' You realise, with a *frisson* of purist horror, that, up and down the country, thousands of people are going to think that this is really what Tolstoy wrote. What do you do? Do you denounce the man and show him to the door? Give him low marks? You don't. Has anything been taken away from Tolstoy? Not a jot. The book is still there, waiting for its next common or uncommon reader. If one remonstrates with Smith, it isn't to preserve Tolstoy from mortal peril, but to put Smith in the way of reading pleasures he seems so far to have missed.

The proper function of criticism, that is to say, is not corrective, preservative or judicial. It is a sociable impulse, aimed at sharing, and communally defining, a prime human pleasure. And in the process, one offers one's own experience of Tolstoy's mind with as much circumstantial candour and as little condescension as one can muster. After all, we most of us have a few Smith-like blunders and blanknesses to our account. There's no call for climbing onto our high horse. *Tristram Shandy*, once more, finds the right note:

> so often has my judgement deceived me in my life, that I always suspect it, right or wrong... For all this, I reverence truth as much as any body; and when it has slipped us, if a man will but take me by the hand, and go quietly and search for it, as for a thing we have both lost, and can neither of us do without – I'll go to the world's end with him: – But I hate disputes...
> (*Tristram Shandy*, V, xi)

As for a thing we have both lost... This sociable, communal function of criticism is one that was taken for granted until well into this century. Read Coleridge, Hazlitt, Lamb, or Bagehot, or Arnold, read Leslie Stephen or A. C. Bradley or Middleton Murry. It might have been one's irritation one was sharing, but one did not lecture, instruct or harangue. The corrective view of criticism assumes – quite wrongly – that it is the critic's business to be correct. In practice (*Truism 6*) one doesn't care tuppence whether he is or not – as long as there is a voice there, notably speaking out of experience.

We don't go on reading Dr Johnson's criticism for the infallibility of his judgement or the precision of his descriptions. I doubt that we even think of ourselves as 'reading criticism' at all when we read him. His account of the metaphysical school hasn't stuck in the gorge of criticism for two hundred years because of its magnificent correctness. But *something has been said.*

Or there is Bradley, who has been dethroned, arraigned, carted and beheaded, but goes on being read. Why not? He can write. Which is more than can be said for some of his deposers.

Or there is Hazlitt – a man who can no more be relied upon to stick by his judgements, than he can be expected to quote his author accurately. I find him using Shakespeare as a stick to beat Ben Jonson with – quite unfairly, as it seems to me:

> [Shakespeare's] humour (so to speak) bubbles, sparkles, and finds its way in all directions, like a natural spring. In Ben Jonson it is, as it were, confined in a leaden cistern, where it stagnates and corrupts; or directed only through certain artificial pipes and conduits to answer a given purpose. The comedy of this author is far from being 'lively, audible, and full of vent': it is for the most part obtuse, obscure, forced, and tedious. He wears out a jest to the last shred and coarsest grain…
> (*Lectures on the English Comic Writers*, Lect I)

It takes nothing from my relish for this essay that I think Hazlitt vastly wrong. I don't even want to refute it. Hazlitt has been frank and manly. He takes it for granted that opinions will diverge: 'There are people who cannot taste olives,' he says, 'and I cannot relish Ben Jonson, though I have taken some pains to do it, and went to the task with every sort of good will.' What more can you ask of a critic, than this candid delivery?

In short, criticism is just another variety of literature – literature about books seen as part of a thinking person's life. One is interested in a critic for the same reason one is interested in a novelist or an essayist – Who is this man? this woman? What do they make of their world? How rich is their experience of it?

Let me try to draw a few threads together. Literature is a communicative circuit – a three-cornered relationship between the writer, the reader, and the world they share. You cannot break into the circuit, abstract something you call 'the literary object', define it, and then, in a wholly separate mental operation, decide how to discuss it. Your discussion itself becomes part of the three-cornered relationship, and will change it, moreover. Whereas a critic's unashamed subjectivity – confessed, exploited, set to work in the prose (as we saw in the case of Hazlitt) – can be met, enjoyed, resisted, a spurious scientism forces us to go a great way about to recover the distorting subjectivity which is hell-bent on obliterating its traces.

One other element the false models of the art-work all have in common: and that is a determination to consider the finer discriminants and subtler emanations of art as refinements which needn't be taken too seriously into account, when defining art's 'essential nature'. In fact the reverse is true. You might almost define art by the remarkable extent to which the subtle, the evanescent, and the unclassifiable lie at the core of its potency. Tolstoy is helpful here:

> Once when correcting a pupil's study, Bryullov just touched it in a few places and the poor dead study immediately became animated. 'Why you only touched it a *tiny bit*, and it is quite another thing!' said one of the pupils. 'Art begins where the *tiny bit* begins,' replied Bryullov, indicating by these words what is most characteristic of art. The remark is true of all the arts, but its justice is particularly noticeable in the performance of music. That musical execution should be artistic, should be art, that is, should carry infection, three chief conditions must be observed… the pitch, the time, and the strength of sound. Musical execution is only then art, only infects, when the sound is neither higher nor lower than it should be, that is, when exactly the infinitely small centre of the required note is taken: when that note is continued exactly as long as it is needed; and when the strength of sound is neither more nor less than is required [. . .] It is the same in all the arts; a tiny bit lighter, a tiny bit darker, a tiny bit higher, lower, to the right or the left – in painting; in dramatic art; a tiny bit omitted, over-emphasised, or exaggerated – in poetry, and there is no contagion. Infection is only obtained when an artist finds those infinitely minute degrees of which a work of art consists, and only to the extent to

which he finds them. And it is quite impossible to teach people by external means to find these minute degrees: they can only be found when a man yields to his feelings. No instructions can make a dancer catch just the time of the music, or a singer or a fiddler take exactly the infinitely minute centre of his note, or a sketcher draw of all possible lines the only right one, or a poet find the only right arrangement of the only suitable words. All this is found only by feeling.

(*What is Art?* Chapter 12)

To which I would like to append some remarks of Matisse's... if I could only find them again. Since I can't, I shall have to paraphrase, hoping that I haven't made them up. He points out that an empty canvas is a neutral entity until the first brush-stroke is applied. Immediately it becomes an active form circumscribing the single stroke. Each successive stroke is both an expression in itself, and also a modification of the expressive form of the unfilled canvas. And each successive stroke is, at the same time, entering into relations with, and changing the force of, every previous stroke. So that, if one bears in mind the infinite possible gradations of colour, the infinite variability of different kinds of stroke – not just in line, but in texture – and if one conceives this network of relations as in some sense *meant* by the painter, it's plain that, by the time the canvas has received a dozen such strokes, the possibilities have become so manifold that no feat of calculation can carry the painter any farther. His 'meaning' must hereafter be intuited, unconscious, and discovered meaning – as he 'yields to the feeling'.

A novel, by the same token, is the end product of billions of such choices among the riches of the language. And if we feel its final form to have some 'inevitable rightness', we're nevertheless in the position of being quite unable to offer any systematic account of that rightness. Which is a good thing because, if we could, we would certainly start talking about it as if it were the product of calculation – and thus falsify it. It follows from this that a criticism which draws attention to the 'rightness' is as much bound to be intuitive, unconscious, and discovered, as the work itself. As critics, we too must 'yield to the feeling'. Give the reins of our imagination up into the hands of the author.

Worryingly subjective? Well, as Shakespeare might have said…

if men were contented to be what they are, there were no fear in subjectivity. It's what we all have in common, after all. All I'm proposing is holding our subjectivities more cheerfully in common, as members of the great Reading Public – instead of enviously, paranoically, and solipsistically as students, scholiasts, experts… critics.

Actually, the cheerfulness depends a good deal upon our believing that the reading public, the common reader positively exists. Whenever I mount this kind of argument I am requested, perfectly reasonably, to produce him/her/it in evidence. I can't. The reading public isn't a verifiable sociological fact. *The reading public is an article of the author's faith which his words alone serve to actualise.* It exists only when it is addressed.

That faith can't of course subsist without some external nourishment. It was the intelligent eye of the common playgoer whose glint Shakespeare caught occasionally from the gallery of the Globe (or was it the pit?). He called this prodigy 'the judicious', and tried to write meeting that eye. And he, the judicious, repaid the compliment (in the nineteenth century, for instance) by meeting regularly, up and down the country, with congenial friends, to read the plays aloud. He existed sufficiently to provide an audience for Coleridge's or Bradley's Shakespeare lectures – which were addressed directly to him. In the eighteenth century, no doubt, he snapped up each new publication of Pope's, and kept *The Rambler* solvent longer than the vagaries of its author would have led him to expect. The classic nineteenth-century realists could rely on him to buy each new instalment and read it aloud to the family. Where is he now? He's around. Reading this.

But the decisive proof of the existence of a reading public lies in a special tone, a calm assurance of being understood, which permeates the writing of the great masters. It's as if the author's faith is efficacious – produces what it believes in.

For instance… there was precious little in late Elizabethan England to justify a belief in the calm, undramatised, self-aware humanity which speaks in the miraculous prose of Shakespeare's *Hamlet*. Yet in an age of ranting histrionic villainy and raving histrionic virtue, of priggish castigators of vice and prurient gloaters over corruption, of comically metaphysical doom-mongers and comically petty theological squabblers, Shakespeare was able to command a stillness to make this voice heard:

I have of late, but wherefore I know not, lost all my mirth, forgone all custom of exercises: and indeed it goes so heavily with my disposition, that this goodly frame the earth, seems to me a sterile promontory, this most excellent Canopy the air, look you, this brave unchanging firmament, this majestical roof fretted with golden fire, why it appeareth nothing to me but a foul and pestilent congregation of vapours. What a piece of work is a man, how noble in reason, how infinite in faculties, in form and moving, how express and admirable in action, how like an Angel in apprehension, how like a God, the paragon of Animals; and yet to me, what is this Quintessence of dust: man delights not me, nor women neither, though by your smiling, you seem to say so.

Until the moment the voice was heard I doubt that anyone could have affirmed with confidence that the late Elizabethan culture contained the possibility of that high and fine equanimity. Yet the moment the voice is heard it becomes plain that this possibility of feeling *must* already exist to be articulated with such assurance. People must be feeling like this and Shakespeare must know it. The sense indeed is just that people always have – that what has been actualised is a permanent register of feeling in the human compass. The miracle is achieved, as I've said, 'by faith'. Yet the faith is no more than an unshakeable assurance that no miracle is required – things are like that, humanity is like that. We may ask how Shakespeare can be so sure, but there's no mistaking the fact that he is.

Take another case: it's one of the fingerprints of Tolstoy's style that, whenever he approaches a crisis of personal intensity in his tale, you get constructions like 'As often happens in such cases...' or 'At such times, men will always...' The appeal to a common reality and a common estimate of that reality could not be made unless Tolstoy knew, with all the certainty of a passionate and un-verifiable faith, that the intelligent reading public was there – his peers and brothers.

And anyone who can put down *Anna Karenina* and feel that he is small, threatened and alone, has not been reading him. At such moments one knows that the great reading public must exist to be addressed, or these things could not have been spoken.

In John Berger's novel *A Painter of our Time*, his expatriate Hungarian artist-protagonist puts it this way:

> Most intellectuals in Europe today wish for strength from their belief that human nature is infinitely varied. It is a vain wish. I gain strength from my knowledge that in any given circumstances most men are the same: it is only the circumstances that are so various. There are other men who want to paint as I do, and in front of our pages or easels, our experiences are common to each of us. There are many brotherhoods without name. And if I had to give a single piece of advice to a young painter, I would remind him of this. Then it would not seem to him so important or tragic or embittering that most of those who talk about art are entirely ignorant.

Brotherhoods without name. They may have no knowledge of each other, no social organ of expression, no monthly journal of propaganda, no distinctive critical methodology, possibly even no sense of corporate identity. They may be 'brotherhoods' composed entirely of sisters. Their hair may be of as many colours as their educational backgrounds. But that's in the nature of the case, since the qualities of judgement, percipience and sensitivity in question are the prerogative of no institution, no educational class, no social grouping, and are bound to be found in a kind of random dispersion across the whole social spectrum.

What happens when the new, the really new work appears, is that it bestows upon these brotherhoods, scattered though they are, the knowledge of their corporate existence and their historical indestructibility. They feel themselves part of a vast continuum and human striving. And they feel honoured by the associates they are conscious of having.

They come into existence – as I've said – the moment they are addressed. And that, if you like, defines the task, not just for the creative writer, but for anyone who chooses to open his or her mouth on the subject of literature. It's a matter of keeping faith with the great past, by addressing the great present which, if it isn't already in existence, we are damn well going to drag into existence.

POETRY

MATTHIAS WEAVER

1995

In hushed downstairs rooms
and unknown alleyways
our laughter firecrackers hitting wet cobbles
and skittering down the lane into the dark

cider on our lips
and light on our feet
this fresh-found music – the best ever – was ours
we moved like dancers and danced like idiots

street lights shining and
curving through empties
we held the future in a careless contempt
we held the instant out like a lit sparkler

and left trails in air
spelled out our names in
orange momentary incandescence, they
vanished instantly and stayed there forever.

NEW THOUGHTS

FATHERS AND SONS

Ian McMillan

My dad, who lived from January 1919 (which seems impossibly long ago and far away) until December 2001, which seems simultaneously impossibly long ago and far away and very close to the day before yesterday, was a big fan of the written and printed word and he passed that love of words and sentences and paragraphs and lines of poetry on to me, and without his gentle and benign influence I wouldn't be the person I am now. He always felt that words, via story and song and anecdote, contained a kind of magic that was released if you breathed into them or wrote them down.

This took the form of gesturing wildly at a letter in the *Trout and Salmon* magazine and reading it out to everyone else in the room because he thought it was brilliant, or singing the beautiful hymn 'The Old Rugged Cross' or that Andy Stewart classic 'Donald Where's Yer Troosers' in a voice that cracked with emotion and often wandered in the general direction of the notes without actually shaking hands with them.

He was born in a cottage called *Falla*, a resonant name that always rang like a bell whenever he said it, just outside a tiny town called Carnwath in Lanarkshire, and he often told me that one of his earliest memories was of running home from school to tell his mother and dad that he'd won a prize in an essay contest with a piece he'd written about The League of Nations, that precursor of the United Nations. I like to imagine the sudden arrival in the house, the breathless excitement, the showing off of the prize, his mother and dad beaming with pride. I have to imagine the prize, too, because he could never quite recall what it was, perhaps because the winning of the prize was greater than the prize itself. I always tell myself that it was a book, a book about all the countries of the world, with their histories and flags and poems and songs, and I imagine him reading it late at night by gaslight (or even candlelight because it was impossibly long ago and far away) and imagining the places at the edges of the map he would go to later in his life, which he did when he joined the navy and sailed towards horizons that were far from Carnwath and *Falla* Cottage.

Two of his favourite books accompanied him on the rolling seas: *The Rubaiyat of Omar Khayyam*, that amazing piece of nineteenth-century faux-exoticism translated into quatrains by Edward Fitzgerald from the work of the Eleventh Century Persian poet. The most famous of the four-liners that make up the book is 'The moving finger writes, and having writ, moves on:/Nor all thy piety and wit/Shall lure it back to cancel half a line,/Nor all thy tears wash out a word of it' and years later when my dad had left the Navy and was working in an office in Sheffield he would often quote it when he was doing the washing up or tying his fishing flies in the tiny conservatory at the back of the house. I wasn't quite sure what it meant but I loved the music of it, which is pretty much my reaction to poetry these days. I don't mind if I don't understand it, but I have to like the poetry of it.

My dad's other favourite book which went with him in his trunk across the South China Sea and the Bay of Biscay was an odd little volume called *The Specialist* by Charles Sale. In essence, this is a book of toilet humour, although really it's much more than that. Charles Sale was an American actor and music-hall turn and *The Specialist* was written in the voice of one Lem Putt (a name that always reminds me of the R Mutt that Marcel Duchamp signed his urinal with) a specialist in the building of

IAN McMILLAN

outdoor toilets. As Putt says 'Gentlemen, you are face to face with the champion privy builder of Sangamon County.' The book, which is only about thirty pages long and reads like a kind of Mark Twain pastiche on the subject of toilet manufacture, made my dad laugh until he cried, his shoulders shaking, his face as red as tomato soup, huge tears rolling down his cheeks to dampen his shirt collar. When, as a cynical teenager, I would ask him to tell me what was so funny about it, he would try and read a paragraph to me but then would laugh so much that it felt like he might require a visit to the outpatients department at the hospital. I've tried to read it many times since and although I can appreciate what it is, it's never made me chortle. And that's another important lesson passed down from father to son: not everybody has to like the same books. It doesn't matter if you like a book that nobody else gets.

I'm reading a book on a late-night train in winter; the train is crowded and overheated and I nod off. I wake up suddenly, two stops past my own, and I look at my reflection in the window and my dad gazes back. The older I get the more I look like him and perhaps the older I get the more I think like him. The moving finger writes, and having writ, moves on. I think I'll dig out his copy of *The Specialist* when I get home at midnight.

Now read on to turn from Ian McMillan, poet and father, to Andrew McMillan, poet and son.

THE POET ON HIS WORK

'FIRST TIME'

Andrew McMillan

first time

before the early times finishing
in old socks or on my own belly
to feel the puddled temporary

warmth there was the first time and before
even that there were the shameful years
of not knowing what it was or why

I'd wake each morning sure
I'd wet myself and find myself dry
but larger than the night before why

the piss fizzed as it hit the bowl
why I always shrank back down to size
what the other boys were laughing at

in school why they would brag how many
times a day they did it why the men
at football games would move their hands like that

ANDREW McMILLAN
© Urszula Soltys

and then that night of discovery
an October holiday Blackpool
because my grandad had recently died

and grandma wanted the family
together the sea couldn't rest
and the empty slots of days dropped down

in front of us each morning one night
when it felt as though the whole hotel
was asleep I reached down and tented

the floral covers on my single bed
a few quiet strokes and then a tide
a pool a bursting through my joggers

and I ran to the bathroom I hadn't
reckoned on the stuff that lingers after
the smell the taut body's fear of being

caught it didn't feel pleasurable
more like learning a secret you could
forget and learn again each day

I went back to bed hoping the night
might dry me as I sank down into
my given task mourning what had passed

So I know it's likely that we've never met, maybe we'll never meet in real life, but having read that poem you know more about me than most of my close friends.

Poetry can't just be a diary entry, or a one-way therapy session for the writer; the job of a poem (if poems have a job at all beyond captivating an audience and 'entertaining' them for a particular length of time, as would be the case with any art) is to get at the 'truth' of something. There's a great Rita-Ann Higgins quote that Selima Hill uses as an epigraph in one of her collections; 'To get to the poetic truth, it is not always necessary to tell the what-actually-happened truth, these times I lie'. So poetry is trying to get at the poetic truth, not the factual truth of something (though of course those two things are often interwoven).

I think poetry has to risk something, in order to come close to being successful. That doesn't mean that a poem has to confess your darkest secret or involve you wrecking your life; it could be something as simple as writing in a form you've never tried before, or challenging the reader to go somewhere they might not have expected to be going. However you do it, there has to be something on the line. There's a lot of solidly good poetry out there, the sort which it's very hard to not like; it's well-crafted, there's a neat simile or two, there's a nice opening-out in the ending line, and yet it's a type of poetry which might often leave one feeling a little flat afterwards. I think poetry needs to do two main things:

a) surprise you as you write it; you shouldn't necessarily know what the ending is going to be when you start writing (this is one of the major differences between writing poetry and writing a murder mystery)

b) make you uncomfortable, or a little afraid; my barometer is that if I'm writing something I know I'd be embarrassed to show my mum, then I must be on to something, because that means there's something in there I'm a little ashamed of, or a little afraid of. Each poet will have their own test, their own idea of what it is that can make a poem vibrate on the page, give it a certain energy.

Despite our desire to carve things up into recognisable chunks, to be able to say this is 'confessional', or 'this is a poetry of the self', and over here, this is something else, those boundaries aren't that clear cut. All poetry is of the poet, it's either their view of something, or their creation of a character, or their wrestling of another language onto the page through translation, or their deliberate removing of themselves from the page, wherein they become present through their absence.

If poetry does begin in something personal, it can't stay there; it can't merely be a status update or a tweet, it has to open out further; it has to give the reader, however implicitly, a sense of why they are being told what they are being told, why are you telling them this thing about your life. So, through synecdoche, it actually becomes about all adolescence, or sexuality, or masculinity or whatever the subject of a particular poem might be. The job of the poet who has chosen the personal as their subject is to look into themselves, find the things that perhaps they feel to be important, and to consider how their presenting of this might not turn further inward, but open up to speak to something of the wider world.

I wrote a book called *physical* that came out in 2015; the poems in it ended up looking at many of the subjects which were (and in many ways still are) pre-occupying me, masculinity, sexuality, class. After that book was off to the publishers, there was that quiet period that I think follows the completion of any artistic project, but then the poems came back again, some of them the splutters of that first book that I needed to be rid of, some of them unsuccessful in their blatant and flagrant attempts to be utterly different to that earlier work, and then I just let the poems come as they wanted to. I've been thinking a lot about childhood, and about adolescence, how it is that we grow into our sexual and physical selves.

'first time' that you've read at the beginning of this article is the first poem I wrote in what turned out to be a sequence of poems about self-exploration and self-discovery, ending with losing my virginity. Normally we might say poems have to be glimpses, capturing a certain moment in time; I realise now, reading over it again, that this poem has a slightly larger sweep to it, beginning before the 'first time' in question. Another thing we might normally say about poems is that they need to be about more than one thing at once, so I can't just have a poem about masturbation, it has to have a wider scope than that, this poem also has in it elements of death, of masculinity, of ageing and of family, and in that sense it isn't really about the self at all, but about these universal themes which come to be shown through a very private and personal act.

The poem is in three-line stanzas, which I favour because of the inherent neatness they bring to the page, suggesting somehow something of excess too, larger than the couplet that our brains are pre-wired to expect. Poetry that is about the self, or takes the self as the starting point, needs to be controlled, it can't simply be splurged onto a page; more often than not the lines here each have nine syllables, so falling slightly short of that expected ten-syllable line, perhaps thinking about something not quite there yet, but getting there. Syllabics and syllables are interesting in that they are very uninteresting, they shouldn't be noticeable to a reader as they move through the poem, except that they might feel the poem appears tight, or structured in a way they might not otherwise feel.

The lack of punctuation is a style I favoured in *physical* as well, and something that I've been developing since I started publishing pamphlets, working with the excellent poet Sarah Hymas. I love the space the lack of punctuation gives, and also feel it somehow more authentic; people never speak in properly punctuated sentences, rather we pause at odd moments, draw in breath and then continue. The spaces, too, are properly counted out, so there are three spaces where a comma might be, and six where a full stop might be – again to give that control where emotion might otherwise take over.

POETRY

THE OLD POEM: JONATHAN SWIFT

Brian Nellist

Stella's Birthday, 1725
ll.15–48

Beauty and wit, too sad a truth!
Have always been confined to youth;
The god of wit and beauty's queen,
He twenty-one and she fifteen,
No poet ever sweetly sung,
Unless he were, like Phoebus, young;
Nor ever nymph inspired to rhyme,
Unless, like Venus, in her prime.
At fifty-six, if this be true,
Am I a poet fit for you?
Or, at the age of forty-three,
Are you a subject fit for me?
Adieu! bright wit, and radiant eyes!
You must be grave and I be wise.
Our fate in vain we would oppose:
But I'll be still your friend in prose:
Esteem and friendship to express
Will not require poetic dress;
And if the Muse deny her aid
To have them sung, they may be said.

But, Stella, say, what evil tongue
Reports you are no longer young;
That Time sits with his scythe to mow
Where erst sat Cupid with his bow;
That half your locks are turn'd to gray?
I'll ne'er believe a word they say.
'Tis true, but let it not be known,
My eyes are somewhat dimmish grown;
For nature, always in the right,
To your decays adapts my sight;
And wrinkles undistinguish'd pass,
For I'm ashamed to use a glass:
And till I see them with these eyes,
Whoever says you have them, lies.

ON 'STELLA'S BIRTHDAY, 1725'
Jonathan Swift (1608-74)
The Works (1734)

Happy three-hundred-and-fiftieth birthday Dr Swift, though I know for you happiness was close to a delusion. When in your younger days you wrote celebratory odes they often seemed awkward and unconvincing, which presumably explained Dryden's reported judgement on them, 'You will never be a poet brother Swift'. In writing prose I know you habitually assume a voice that by implication discredits itself, innocence is perceived as self-deception and enthusiasm as moral blindness. But when you returned to Ireland after your involvement with English politics you were with Esther Johnson whom you'd first met at Moor Park in the old days with Sir William Temple. In your poems you usually drop the mask adopted in the prose satires though you give your closest female friend the unwontedly romantic name of Stella. But then even in your severest satires I detect often a lightness of touch, indeed a playfulness (am I right?) which paradoxically, in this birthday poem, allows a voice of feeling to be heard. Maybe here that's because of your horror of ageing; I'm thinking of the Struldbrugs in the third of Gulliver's voyages and more particularly the lines 'On the Death of Dr Swift', undoubtedly (don't be angry), your greatest poem. What I so admire in this case though is your willingness to turn these disabilities to advantage. If your eyes are failing at least they enable you to see Stella as she once was. How witty in the serious sense that you admit the loss of the old inspiration 'Adieu! bright wit, and radiant eyes' and commit yourself henceforth to prose, yet in the next verse vindicate your undying vitality in verse. Happy for once to be lied to by your eyes since how can you tell it's an untruth after all? 'Trust nature', indeed; simplicity is for such a complicated mind best in the end. How wonderfully you establish the benefits of uncertainty, and how it summons your faith that for you Stella never can change. Fancy you, you angry man, on those grounds writing such a moving and original love poem.

PS Sorry to be late, as usual I'm afraid, for your anniversary

INTERVIEW

NOT ACTING, JUST BEING

Craig Parkinson in conversation with Fiona Magee

*Actor, Craig Parkinson, 41, grew up in Blackpool and went to drama school in London. He is known for his roles on TV, such as Shaun in E4's **Misfits** and DI Cottan – aka 'The Caddy' – in BBC's **Line of Duty**. He has also appeared in several independent films, such as Samantha Morton's **The Unloved** and Chris Morris' **Four Lions**.*

*Always a fan of podcasts, Craig (together with producer Thomas Griffin) recently created **Two Shot Podcast** – a podcast about acting which features a different guest each time in a sit-down with Craig, discussing the, 'highs and sometimes extreme lows of becoming and being an actor'.*

Past guests have included Vicky McClure, Sanjeev Bhaskar, Tamzin Outhwaite and Neil Morrissey, amongst others. Twenty episodes have been recorded so far, with many more planned for 2018.

He lives in the Cotswolds with his wife – actor Susan Lynch – and son.

How did **Two Shot Podcast** come about?

I had trouble sleeping one night so I got up to make a brew and I started reading this piece in the paper about how certain types of kids can't afford to train at drama school because it's so expensive – and I thought, 'This needs to be addressed'. Because if only the privileged and a certain class and type of young person can afford to go to drama school, then obviously you only get that coming out.

I was thinking, 'Who's speaking to the *other* kids?' I wanted to open things up a bit and make a difference, get those other voices – the ones that aren't usually represented – out there.

I was already a big fan of podcasts and I've been acting now for twenty years and I thought, 'I know quite a lot of people in the business, I could do something here'.

Did you go to drama school yourself?

I did, yeah. I begged and battered the door down to win a grant to Blackpool and The Fylde College and then I went to Mountview Academy of Theatre Arts in London. I was a slight tear-away at school, didn't enjoy it that much. It was the deputy head who got me into acting; he'd written a play – it was fantastic, a kind of Elizabethan time-travel comedy – and he took me aside and said, 'Look, you've got to stop skipping class and you *have* to be in this play'. It was amazing – I got on stage and started making people laugh; all of a sudden I went, 'Oh! I like this!'.

I don't regret going to drama school at all, but part of the reason behind the podcast is to say – 'Look, if you've got a dream or something you want to be positive about, don't let anyone tell you that you can't do it. There's always a way, even if you don't go through drama school'.

I've worked with lots of actors over the years who haven't trained, and didn't go through that traditional route and I think they bring a rawness and a realness – they're not 'acting' they are just *being*. Which is what we as actors are constantly trying to do; they've already got it because they're not being told anything different.

How did you choose your guests?

First of all, it's who says yes! Right at the start me and Griff, the producer, met up in a pub in Manchester and talked about what shape it would take and who we'd want to be on it. It started off with people I knew pretty well, but even then I'd never sat down with them and chatted for an hour – you very rarely do, do you? When do you ever sit down with one person and make it all about that other person?

*The first episode is with Vicky McClure – your co-actor in **Line of Duty** – isn't it?*

Yes and I was really nervous, even though Vicki's a really close friend of mine. We go out together and chat all the time, but this was a completely different vibe. I was conscious, because I'm a big fan of podcasts, that I didn't want it to be like anything else out there. And I didn't want to act or be any sort of personality on it or for it to turn around and be about me in any way. Because in some interviews that does happen: you know the kind of thing – 'Oh it's funny you should say that because when I was doing such and such....'

I've heard that sort of interview and as a listener I just go 'No!' It's narcissistic, it puts me off, the walls come down and I don't want to listen to you ever again.

Two Shot Podcast is a very unstructured chat, usually over a brew, and the people who are on are just *them*. That's why it gets such a strong reaction, I think.

*You recently made it into **The Observer**'s Top 10 Podcasts of 2017! What is it that listeners are responding to, do you think?*

I think it's because the guests are very open and honest – they are not putting on a front or being 'an actor', they're going, 'Look, yeah, I had a shit time as a kid, I was bullied, I never really fitted in'. It's not a podcast all about, 'Oh look at the despair and terrible upbringing I've had but I've turned my life around'; those stories do come up but so do other stories about fantastic childhoods and being very supported. Either way, people are talking about real life. Hopefully the feel of it is a bit like two pals chatting down the pub, and you just happen to be on the next table listening – not in a weird way, just overhearing.

Are there things you are able to draw on from your life in acting, that have helped you with the podcasts?

Possibly something to do with listening. Acting is a lot about listening; you're listening and watching all the time – you see things out on the street in daily life and you kind of put those in your 'actor backpack' because you never know when you could use them. We always start from the same basic place – if you're in a scene with somebody you really *listen* to what they're saying and then react accordingly, as though that's the first time you've heard this information.

But it's more like there's a whole new set of skills that I'm learning to do and I absolutely adore that. God, it's been such a journey.

A journey how?

I feel like I've learnt loads about me, by it *not* being about me. Thinking about what I just said about listening – I've definitely learnt to be a *better* listener. In real life, we talk over each other a lot because we're all scrambling for our view or our voice to be heard; just stop.

And with the podcast, I'm not being a character. I've acted for twenty years and constantly played different characters – there's something quite vulnerable about being myself. It's scary.

*How is it **not** like acting?*

What we don't have as actors is control. We're constantly at the beck and call of other people – 'Yes, you've got that job', 'No you haven't got that job', 'Do it like this', 'Do it like that', 'Hurry up!'.

You can do twenty takes of a scene and you'll know which one you're happy with; whether they use that one in the edit is not up to you, not your job.

What I wanted to do was have complete control over something I've made and this seemed to be the right outlet. We've got complete control about what we want to talk about, it can last half an hour or nearly two hours, and there's *no-one telling us what to do*.

Do you set yourself any 'rules' for the interviews?

Only one really, which is that we don't really talk about jobs. If we did that it would turn into some kind of press interview or be a bit insular. If people are interested in that there's loads of it on the internet – I don't want to be rehashing something.

I never go into any episode with any expectation. People might not want to talk about certain things and might shut things down, and they have done, but you know, I'm not an investigative journalist. I'm just an actor who started a podcast who's interested in other people and wants other stories to get out there. So when something emotional does happen in an episode it kind of knocks me for six really. I'm as much in this conversation as the people who are listening.

What kind of 'something emotional' do you mean?

I've found stuff out about people I know very well – or thought I knew very well – just by sitting down with them and having that nice intimate atmosphere.

There was one I did with an actor called Lauren Socha: Lauren had a very difficult upbringing, and I knew that, because I'd worked with her twice. She puts on a very big front – she'd sooner fight first and ask questions later which tends to rub people up the wrong way or get her into trouble. And it did. She had great success, won a BAFTA and then not long after that it all got a bit crazy for her, she ended up getting arrested and got dropped from the series (*Misfits*) she was in. She's slowly but surely building herself back up. I've known her for over ten years and she got very upset in the interview – which shocked her. She said, 'It's like bloody therapy this!'

It's not my intention, and I would never want to exploit anybody, but you know, we talk about the human condition; we talk about people as humans, not as 'actors'.

And the plan is now to also record some non-actors?

Yes, in 2018 we're opening the podcast up to all different creative types. I've just done two initial ones with musicians and we've got a writer, a director, a poet. What's become apparent is that, of course, actors are listening to the podcast, but there are loads of people who aren't actors that are really getting something out of it. People usually listen to podcasts when they're doing something else – commuting, at the gym, cleaning up (in my case) – but it's a peculiarly intimate way of listening. It's in your ears – just you and the person who's telling their story.

Yes, it's about story, isn't it?

After twenty years as an actor, when I receive a script, I know what's a good story and what isn't.

With good writing you get inside the mind of somebody else. Some scripts are incredible to read because once you unlock a page, you're in that world, picturing everything – that's what great writing does. The drama I did a few years ago, *Line of Duty*, I remember reading the script of the first episode, getting to the end, gasping and grabbing episode two straight away, because I needed to know.

On the other hand, there are things I read that I can't get past: last week I read six episodes of a new adaptation of a classic piece of literature and… I was really not impressed! I could tell, as a story, it just didn't work. Just reading the lines of dialogue, as an actor, hearing them in my head… I was thinking, 'This seems really out of place' and, 'Why has that character got to that point in episode two? He's put all his cards on the table and we've got another four hours of his journey to go'.

And it's important to know where to *end* a story. With the podcast, sometimes you could just go on, but I've learnt how to try and end it neatly. If we are dealing with something that's quite a sensitive story, there'll be a moment of uplift or positivity – don't get me wrong, I never want to sugar coat it or have some kind of formula, but I do want to end it at a point where it feels like, ok, that's something for you as a listener to take away somehow.

*Will we be hearing **your** story?*

That's never, ever going to happen! It's not why I started it. I am trying to get other voices out there, not my own. When someone says, at the end, 'Oh I really enjoyed that, I didn't expect that would happen', then I just feel a real sense of pride that they've got as much out of it as hopefully the listener has out of it.

It's not like a piece of theatre where you're like, 'Oh, we'll go back to it tomorrow night and see what we can change' and it's not like a TV show where you do a take and you go 'Right, the next time we do it, we'll try this'. It's something that two people are sharing in that moment – we can't repeat it, it's there, done.

MICHAEL BALOGUN

AND CRAIG PARKINSON

55

Craig and producer Griff travel up and down the UK to talk to actors who have a interesting story to share about the how, why, where and when of their journey into the industry. They have sat down with some of the finest in the business and have heard some incredibly moving, absorbing and insightful tales of misspent childhoods, drama-school dropouts, lucky breaks and flunked auditions.

One such story is that of recent RADA graduate Michael Balogun.

TWO SHOT PODCAST

Michael Balogun

*Actor **Michael Balogun**, 33, grew up in South London. He spent much of his younger life in and out of prison, until he took up a place at RADA. Graduating after three years training, his first job was playing the character Shaun in the nationwide tour of **People, Places and Things** – a play by the British playwright Duncan Macmillan, widely praised by critics for its depiction of addiction. He will shortly take up his first TV role.*

*His **Two Shot Podcast** interview with Craig Parkinson can be found at https:// twoshotpod.podbean.com/e/tsp017-michael-balogun/*

Reading was always in me. At Primary School I loved books – you had your little reading record to fill in, I loved all that. I read on my own, a lot. No-one read to me – never had a bedtime story; it wasn't that kind of household. I could just get lost in a story and go to another world for a couple of hours and just be there.

Then my mum got nicked and went to prison and I started secondary school, and life went a bit down the wrong path.

Reading wasn't a priority for me anymore. I was more focused on things I could see and touch; more focused on getting clothes and money and all that – survival took over. And the kind of people I started associating with – to be walking around with a book in your hand?! You didn't do it. The kind of schools that I went to, it wasn't cool to be someone walking around with flippin Shakespeare or whatever. You know what I'm saying?

I believe that the most important things you have as a human being are things that you *can't* really see and touch – your imagination, your feelings, your emotions, your thoughts, your spirit, your soul. And as a child, you're more in tune with those things – you're more in tune with *yourself*. And then as you grow up and get older you start to notice all this stuff outside and around you and *that* becomes more important and gets in the way; what other people think of you, how you look, what kind of clothes you wear, what kind of social group you are in – all these kind of things start kicking in around secondary school. You forget about those other things that moved you as a child. Obviously if you're lucky enough to come from a family and a background that keeps that kind of flow going, then you're alright. But I wasn't that lucky.

So I stopped reading. Well, almost. Every now and again I'd read something to myself, because I always loved English, even at secondary school, it was the one class that I liked – but I kept that side of myself hidden.

Then I went to prison, for my first sentence, and I fell in love with reading again. When you're in prison, those things that appealed to you outside – how you dress, the world around you, the people you're associating with, the places you go – that's taken away. There's no shops, no nice cars, no partying – all of that stuff is gone. So you are kind of back to square one again, you're back to *yourself*. You're in this cell, alone, and for some reason, the creative side of you comes a bit closer to the surface.

So when I read a book in prison, compared to when I read on the outside, I could see the images more vividly, because there's not a lot of distraction. You get that feeling of being lost in it again, just like when you are a kid.

Number one, reading was a way of killing time but more than that, it was a way of taking the bars off the windows: when you're in a book, you're *in* it, especially in prison – if it's a good story, you forget everything else.

At first I was reading a lot of black literature and black history – I read about Malcolm X, Martin Luther King, books about Ancient Eygpt. I did read a lot of books about gangsters and all that as well, but I *know* about that, I've lived it, so it got to the point where I wanted to read something completely different. I started to realise that knowledge, just knowing some stuff, is more important than the materialistic things I had been really into.

I was in and out of prison a few times – at one point I was in HMP Brixton and I started working at the CLINKS restaurant there and through that, because it was a Cat D (open) prison, I got a position working in the bar at RADA – that's how I first came across it – but I tried to bring a phone back into the prison and I got caught, so they shipped me out to HMP Elmley, a normal closed-condition prison and I got in a bad way.

I was suffering from mental health issues, I was smoking a lot of spice, couldn't sleep. And one day, I said to myself, 'If I don't figure out, tonight, what I'm going to do with my life, I'm going to kill myself'. It was about five-o-clock in the afternoon and I decided I'd give myself twelve hours to figure something out, and if I didn't, that was it. I made a noose and I just closed my eyes and started thinking about everything. That's when the universe – or whatever it was – gave me the idea about acting.

It was strange – the *next day* this lady came into the prison and said, 'I work for CARATS (Counselling, Assessment, Referal, Advice and Throughcare) and I'm part of the mental health team at the prison and officers are concerned about you and thinking of maybe sectioning you' – I was doing a lot of crazy things at the time – and I was like 'No, I'm fine now. I know I'm fine. I want to be an actor'. She was like 'Whoa, Michael', she thought my mind was definitely gone.

And I said, 'No, I'm being genuinely serious, I'm fine now. I'm not smoking anymore, I'm going to be an actor.' And something in the way I said it to her, made her believe me.

She said, 'Well, that's interesting, because if you are serious… I am also a part-time drama teacher'.

She started bringing in plays for me to read, just dropping them off – *Romeo and Juliet*, *The Importance of Being Earnest*. That was the first time I'd read plays and I struggled. *King Lear* was the one – I read it three times.

The first time I was like, *What?!* I kind of knew what was going on – this man's going a bit crazy, two of his daughters seem a bit dodgy, one of them is really nice and for some reason, because she's telling the truth he's banished her because he doesn't want to hear the truth. And he's got his hundred knights around him and he's trying to throw his weight around but no-one is respecting him. But it was not easy. I was like, 'Who's this fool? What's with the way they're speaking?' The language – it's so hard to understand but at the same time, I got a sense of what was happening. Words are just a symbol for something else, aren't they? They're just symbols for feelings and thoughts and emotions – things that we've created as human beings as an extension of what's going on inside. And there is this thing about words – there is an energy to them – it was like, in *King Lear* I could read that energy between the lines.

When you read a book, you're kind of going inside that person's mind, aren't you? I'd be like, 'Wow, I've just read Shakespeare' and 'I've just been inside Charles Dickens' mind!' And at the same time you're kind of feeding your own mind and making it bigger. It's not like watching a movie where the images of what you're watching are already all there: you have to do all the work, so it kind of makes you the director, the actor, the set designer – all these roles that you fill out with your imagination.

This idea that I wanted to be an actor – it charged me up with enthusiasm. I kind of dived in and started reading like a mad man! I was trying to fix myself in my own weird way. I'd go to the library and get my maximum limit of books – five – and I'd come out with this pile and I had all this time; I was reading a book a day. And I could feel the difference in myself. I decided I had to read the classics, 'I need to read *War and Peace*, I need to read *Pride and Prejudice*', so I started reading those kinds of books and just the *food* of them… you don't actually know what it's doing inside of you when you're reading a book but it's *in* there, it enriches you. And when you need it, it can come out.

When I got released, I auditioned for RADA, and that period of time of reading all those books, it helped me. I remember I got through to the fourth round, which is when you're working with other people in scenes and doing monologues and all these things, and the play was set around 1910: me being me, a certain type of person, from South London, having to play this guy from that period who was a bit on the sensitive side. The teacher said,

MICHAEL BALOGUN

60

'Michael, the thing that made me see what you could do was that I know you've not been brought up around that kind of literature, and I know you've not come from that kind of background, but you seem to be able to go into that place.' And it was partly because of those books I read – I was able to connect to things that perhaps people wouldn't have expected me to.

I was at RADA for three years and I'm not going to lie to you, I struggled a lot. I'd never done any acting before and it wasn't my kind of environment – it was very middle class and I found it hard at first to be myself there. I'm not the smartest person intellectually, I love to read but I never went to college or university, I was a bit older than everyone else there and I had this inferiority complex for the first year and a half. I held myself back. Everyone else had been doing that kind of thing already for years, and then there was me, thinking, 'I don't even know if I *can* act'. But then I started to think, I bring something – I bring *this*, this is who I am and I've got to use what I've got.

You know what was funny? One of the first things I had to do was play the part of King Lear!

When I read it in prison, the lines Edmund says in Act 1, Scene 2, really spoke to me. He speaks about how his father doesn't treat him right because he's a bastard. I remembered how I was so angry when I was younger. It was like I was against the people around me because I'd be thinking, 'You've got everything – you've got your mum, you've got your dad' and on parents' evening their parents would turn up. I had no-one turning up. I was very depressed as a child. I just thought, 'Fuck it' and started doing my own thing.

And then when I played King Lear, I identified with him as well, you know? He can't see the error of his ways, he ends up going through the mill and only gets to see where he went wrong when it is too late.

But things are different for me now. I just want to work – a movie, TV series, theatre, it's all good. This is the first thing that I've found in my life that's kept me on the straight and narrow; the first thing that unites all the different things that I'm into – I love it. There's nothing more exciting than being on a stage, acting, and you know that anything can go wrong at any minute. It reminds me of crime. I get that same buzz that I used to get when I was doing stupid things. Now it's legal, and people are enjoying it and people are paying to see it.

King Lear (Act 1, scene 2)

Enter EDMUND the bastard, with a letter

EDMUND
Thou, nature, art my goddess. To thy law
My services are bound. Wherefore should I
Stand in the plague of custom and permit
The curiosity of nations to deprive me
For that I am some twelve or fourteen moonshines
Lag of a brother? Why 'bastard'? Wherefore 'base'?
When my dimensions are as well compact,
My mind as generous, and my shape as true
As honest madam's issue? Why brand they us
With 'base,' with 'baseness,' 'bastardy,' 'base,' 'base'—
Who in the lusty stealth of nature take
More composition and fierce quality
Than doth within a dull, stale, tirèd bed
Go to th' creating a whole tribe of fops
Got 'tween a sleep and wake? Well then,
Legitimate Edgar, I must have your land.
Our father's love is to the bastard Edmund
As to the legitimate.—Fine word, 'legitimate'!—
Well, my legitimate, if this letter speed
And my invention thrive, Edmund the base
Shall top th' legitimate. I grow, I prosper.
Now, gods, stand up for bastards!

Michael Balogun is represented by Lesley Duff (Director) at Diamond Management 020 7631-0400
ld@diman.co.uk

You can find and follow the podcast at https://twoshotpod.podbean.com where you can also subscribe and/or make a donation to the running costs of the show by becoming a patron – receiving bonus pictures, video and audio in return.

POETRY

JOHN LEVETT

A Pair of Boots

I found a pair of steel-capped boots
My father lent me eight years back
'For a week or two, till the snow melts'
'And the thin ice' I murmured 'cracks.'
They were too large, spring ice turned black
And years flew past snowdrift by drift.
'You can keep them now he's gone,' Mum said,
Tongue-tied, tight-laced, a funeral gift.

I wore them once, for love, for duty,
Struck sparks and banged around until,
Not big enough to fill them properly,
I turned to what I could fulfill
And gave them to the Hospice shop
Where, brushed up like a spruced heirloom,
With a Gift Aid code and a £5 tag
They stood guard by the changing room.

I peered in past an angled window,
Its chrome-braced shelves of bric-a-brac,
And in each flared, sun-thrown reflection
My grin brought his grin briefly back
As, dustily, I glimpsed my father
Slipped toe-tagged from his stainless drawer,
Marched barefoot from his funeral parlour,
Come for his boots through the swung glass door.

NEW FICTION AND OLD

FICTION

BURNING BUSH

Frank Cottrell Boyce

They were a family from the war zone and they had managed to stay together all the way to the coast. Now they were waiting in a narrow cove for the boat to appear. They didn't know the name of the cove. There was no Moon and the clouds were low. They could sense that there were others waiting there when they arrived but they did not know who or how many. Every now and then a wave smashed on the rocks and the rocks clattered as the sea pulled the wave back into itself. During one of these commotions the Father said quietly, 'These others might be police or worse. Keep quiet. We won't let anyone know we are here until we have to.'

In the quiet between the waves, though, the boy said out loud, 'We're not police if that's what you're worried about. We're just waiting for the boat like you all.' There was a ripple of answering sniggers. The darkness relaxed and even grew a little lighter, though that was surely because their eyes were getting used to it.

The boy had been acting this way more and more in the last few days – taking things into his own hands, going over the heads of the Mother and the Father.

At first the Father had been in charge. It was his idea to leave the city. Before the war closed the airports, he had been a steward on the national airline. He had served food in the air above dozens of countries and slept in hotels across the World. He knew that the war was not something that had to be endured. Anyone could walk away from it as long as they were not scared. Just a few hours away from this city, he said, families like ours are queueing at breakfast buffets, choosing between Healthy Options and Treat Yourself.

The Mother had objected. The war would not go on forever. Who were these people anyway that they should make her run away from the home she had built and from her family, not to mention her study group.

The Father had said yes it was true the war would not go on forever. They could leave now, today, and pay Ali to look after the house while they were gone. It would be like going on holiday. If they didn't go, who knows, the boy might get caught up in the fighting, and the girl might be kidnapped.

The Mother agreed to go but she had held on to her unhappiness because it gave her bargaining power. She used this to insist that they take the big car – the SUV – and load it with all her most precious things, mainly electrical goods, family photographs and shoes. The children had seen her victory as theirs and they had insisted on XBoxes, tablets and the SingStar karaoke machine.

At the city gates, they were stopped by a group of young militia who made them empty the car onto the pavement. They took all the electrical goods for reasons of security. 'It looks like a SingStar,' one admitted, 'but how do I know it's not a bomb?' They took the family photographs – in their silver frames – 'to help with identification.' Then they drained the petrol from the car as a contribution to the ongoing struggle for the security of the people.

When they got to the next town the man who kept the garage shook his head. He had only a little petrol and he wouldn't sell it. They would be best to sell the car as it was big and thirsty and desirable and would attract the wrong sort of attention. Even the Mother now had to admit this was the case. The man with the garage said he would buy it off them. He knew a farmer who was looking for such a car. He said a price.

'What?!?' shrieked the Mother. 'One tyre costs more than that.'

'Yes but then a tyre might be useful,' said the man. 'The car though is a burden. The farmer I am thinking only wants it as a place to keep chickens.'

'You're offering us the price of one tyre,' said the Father. 'But the car has five tyres.'

'True,' admitted the man and he paid them five times his starting offer. So they sold the car for the price of five tyres.

It was painful when two days later the man passed on the road, driving their car – music blasting out, dogs on the back seat, obviously going hunting.

The Mother called the Father a fool for letting it go so cheap.

The Father called the Mother a fool for insisting on bringing it with them and even more for loading it with their valuables. All of which now were gone.

When she cried, the Father told her not to. From the next town they would take a bus North to the border. Once they were out of the war zone, he would call the bank, move their savings hire a car and drive them all to Europe, the land of education, freedom, healthy options and spoil yourself.

It was during this conversation – which happened on the bus they took to a small town on the edge of the desert – that the boy realised that his parents were no longer in control, and possibly did not understand the situation they were in.

In the small town on the edge of the desert, the square was packed with people. It smelled of urine and tobacco. The youngest daughter climbed onto the Father's shoulders to see better. The Mother asked a policeman is this a revolution? The policeman said that no it was not a revolution, it was people waiting for the next bus North. There were four thousand people in the square. Each bus carried fifty people. There were four buses a day. It was possible to get a ticket for a few days time if you could find someone from the bus company and pay them a big enough bribe. Always assuming the buses would still be running. The drivers were getting weary and some were refusing to drive. Also there were stories of people posing as employees of the bus company and selling fake tickets.

This is when the boy began to take charge. For hundreds of years, he said, people have walked across the desert from here. This is why the town began – so that people could stock up on water and food before making the walk across the desert. It was less than thirty miles. It could be done in two days. Our forefathers did it. So can we.

The Father said no. The Mother said – are we going to listen to the man who sold our car for the price of five tyres?

The Father said, 'Are we going to listen to this woman who made you bring your SingStar and family photographs into a war zone so that any teenager with an automatic weapon could take them from you?'

The boy took his sister away; they bought water and big linen sheets to make shade. We will walk, he said.

The Mother had wanted to hire a guide but the way was easy to see. It was marked by thousands of empty water bottles. Some of them had melted and fused into each other making a long trail that shone with a cold, dead light, as though a massive slug had passed that way. They followed it until the heat was unbearable, then made a shade out of the sheets and waited for the Sun to sink a little. When they stood up the Mother collapsed. They discovered that she had drunk no water because she did not want to urinate where there was no toilet. They made her drink. The Father held the sheets while she urinated behind them. He told her that he had visited the town on the coast for a conference once. It was surrounded by lemon groves and the people there were good.

But when they came to the coast, the town could not be seen behind placards, barbed wire and armoured vehicles. They were herded into the camp.

The camp was bigger than the town.

At the beginning of the war, an agency had provided some tents but they had run out after the first few days. The tents had been delivered in large wooden boxes and some people slept in these. These too were all occupied. There were no toilets. The main reason that people left their farms and homes was to protect their children. Nearly everyone in the camp had children. There were hundreds of children. Someone had set up a school. The older ones taught the younger ones. The boy and his sister turned out to be quick to learn languages. She learnt German and some Greek. Boys played football. The Mother was worried that the children would get lost.

The son borrowed a bicycle and rode all around the camp. He drew a map for the others. He scavenged enough waste to make a shelter.

They had been there for six weeks when the Father finally found a man from the Hegari Happy Landings Company who would take them across the Isthmus in a boat. Once they landed all would be well. The man took you to an agent. You paid the money to the agent. He gave you a number to ring. When you were safe on the other side, you rang the number. The Hegari Happy Landings Company wouldn't get their money until you rang that number, until you were safe. It was proof that they didn't want you to drown. The crossing was just two hours.

The Mother was excited about the crossing. She had been on boats before. She could swim well. She was unhappy they had to buy condoms to put their cash and cards and mobile phones in to save them from getting wet.

The boy said the camp was not a good place but it was not dangerous like the sea. Maybe they could stay here. The war could not go on forever.

I used to believe that the war could not go on forever, said the Father. I don't believe that any more. Maybe this war will go on forever. No one knows what it's for. No one knows how to end it. All we can do is escape.

And this is how they came to be in the cove when the headlights of a truck lit up the rocks. Silhouettes scrambled to hide. Then reappeared when they saw the truck was pulling an inflatable boat. They crowded around it.

The Father said to hurry or they would lose their place.

'That's a lot of people,' said the boy. 'That's too many people.' But his Mother and his sisters were already in the inflatable and the truck was already dragging the inflatable into the sea.

No one spoke.

They were all praying.

The man at the helm was wearing a good life jacket and a hat pulled down to his eyes. When they passed the headland and were out on the open sea, there was some light from the Moon. The man at the helm said nothing but slid noiselessly over the side and started to swim back towards the rocks. At first the people thought he had fallen in. They called to him and held out their hands to him but soon they saw that he was calmly swimming away from them towards the shore. He had abandoned them.

The Father shouted to everyone to stay calm. 'We have only to go in a straight line. The islands are so near and the people there will welcome us.'

Something inside the boy broke then. He was not sure what it meant. He just felt something snap in his heart.

He put his hand under his sister's chin and rolled them both backwards into the water. He swam on his back to the shore, keeping his hand there. All the way he could hear the panic, the shouting and the prayers coming from the inflatable boat. He had given up on everyone in the boat. It was just him and his sister now.

When they got to the beach the man who had abandoned them was still there. He even nodded to the children before getting into the truck as it backed out of the cove.

His sister kept calling for their Mother and asking him to go back for her. 'They're too far away. If they land safely they will ring us in a few hours,' said the boy, but only to make her stop crying. He was to find that he felt strangely elated and strong. He had rescued Amira. He was sure of that. His head filled up with plans for making money, for getting to Europe. Just the two of them. 'Me and you, Amira,' he said, taking her hand and leading her back towards the camp.

They had left the camp through a gap in the fence. They were almost back there when they saw the fire. An olive grove had been bulldozed to make room for the camp. One of the uprooted trees was on fire. That is to say there were leaves of fire fluttering along its branches and a great blossom of fire blazing in its bole. But the tree was not burning. The boy walked closer. 'What's going on?' he said.

'You would know if you'd read the Qu'ran,' said the fire. There was no question that it was the fire that was speaking. 'I am that fire that Moses saw.'

'Yeah? Then why are you speaking German?' said the boy.

'I am what I am,' said the fire. 'Take your shoes off.'

'Nein,' said the boy and walked away. The fire died down. The boy turned back to the tree. The fire rose up again. Turned away, it went down. Back again it rose up. His little sister laughed.

The fire said, 'All will be well.'

It was because it made his sister happy that the boy decided to stay by the fire.

The people nearest the fence were the first to know about the fire that never went out, the fire that did not burn the tree, the fire that supposedly spoke to the boy. Soon the whole camp knew. They forced the fence. Police in armoured vehicles were on the scene immediately, ready to force them back through the gap. But when the police saw that they only wanted to sit by the fire and not storm the town, they pulled back and made a cordon. When they saw that the fire did not burn the tree, some of the officers crept forward. When their shifts were over many did not go home but waited around to see what would happen.

There were those in the town who called the fire a major public order problem. The watching crowd was a clever new kind of incursion. A land grab by the camp. Their problem was that every time they sent any official in to disperse the crowd, the officials would end up joining the crowd. They were intrigued by the unburning fire. They wanted to know what it was saying to the boy.

The boy mostly refused to disclose what the fire was saying. He was partly afraid that the crowd would be disappointed. The truth was that the fire mostly gave little talks about German cultural life. The sister sat at his side, nodding. She seemed genuinely interested in the history of reunification and the comedy career of Otto Waalkes. He sometimes spoke to the fire, asking it if there was some way he could monetise the situation.

'When you say monetise,' said the fire, 'do you mean exploit? For your own gain?'

'Yes. Come on. There must be.'

Just then someone noticed that there was free Wi-Fi all across the fire's glow zone. People crowded in to FaceTime and Skype their relatives in the places they had fled, or the places they were fleeing too. The more people crowded in, the brighter the fire glowed and the wider the Wi-Fi zone spread. Faces of family flickered like flames around the great fire. It felt like the whole people who had been scattered by the war were gathered again here, around this camp fire. The network's name was S.

The boy's phone never rang. Nor did his sister's. He knew that his parents had been lost.

No one wanted to leave the fire. The crowd became a public order problem. The police came to try to move the people back into the camp but they were too many.

The fire told the boy to speak to the leaders of the nations and tell them to let the people go. The boy said he didn't know the leaders of any nations and besides his credit was low. His phone rang. It was Merkel. There was a slightly awkward conversation. She thought she had called her hairdresser by mistake. He told her he was talking on behalf of all the peoples. After that Cameron rang and then insisted he hadn't rung. He hung up but then phoned again and this continued until the boy blocked Cameron.

'You will FaceTime,' said the fire, 'All the peoples of the Europe.'

The fire patched him into the semi-final of the *Great British Bake Off*. His face – staring, solemn and silent – completely obliterated the show stopper round. The Prime Minister called this a new and twisted form of terrorism. Also an insult to Mary Berry. In Germany he ruined everyone's Sunday sleep-in by staring out from *Sendung Mit Maus*. He stared out too from the *Samantha Oops Summer Special* and the Turkish version of *The Voice*.

He hadn't been able to think of anything to say. He just stared with his big, pleading eyes which had seen so much.

'That was embarrassing,' he said to the fire. 'No,' said the fire. 'That was important. It is not about words or arguments. It is about people, just the fact of people. A boy's youth. An old person's age. A child's vulnerability, an adult's ability. What is the Truth? I am the Truth. And through me, you are the Truth. All of you.' It was twilight then. As far as you could see there were faces, faces on screens and faces lit by the faces on the screens, talking, laughing, about nothing much, a field of bright flowers feeding on the fire's free Wi-Fi. It seemed to him as if all the faces in human history were there except those of the Father and the Mother. His sister leaned into him and held his hand.

That's when they were declared an international security issue. An attempt to establish a nation within another nation's borders. The United Nations passed a resolution agreeing that any means possible could be used for their dispersal.

'Tell them that if they do not embrace you I will send plagues against them,' said the fire.

'Don't do that,' said the boy. 'It'll only make things worse.'

But the fire patched him into the Champions' League Final and – for something to say – he said what the fire had said, 'You will launch drones against us and you will wish that you had not. Your vehicles will be lost. Your people will cease to obey you.'

A drone was launched against the people of the fire. They saw it pass over their heads and they were not afraid. It turned and headed for the city and wherever it passed over military installations, other drone rose up to join it. It flew over the sea, across Greece and into Germany, and all the way great flocks of drones rushed up to join it – not only military drones but also drones from sports events and amateur photographers – until the drones were like a cloud blocking out the Sun wherever it passed. The drone cloud hovered over Berlin. Over London. Over Paris.

Then it plunged into the sea. 'Your drones were plunged into the sea,' said the boy, 'because of my pleading. I have saved your cities now let us in.'

Emergency committees across Europe had already launched a land attack from bases in Turkey.

'What will happen?' asked the little sister.

'I plunged Pharaoh's army into the sea,' said the fire.

'Oh don't do that,' pleaded the little sister. 'Dolphins!'

For her sake therefore the fire took over the GPS of the nations and caused a pan-European traffic jam which rendered every road unpassable.

'Now,' said the fire, 'I will lead you.'

And the fire moved.

And the people were afraid.

The boy and his sister followed the fire and the people followed the boy and his sister, and the fire and the boy and his sister lead them all to the little cove.

And this was on TV so that the Nations beheld a people walking, following the fire.

And the fire lead them to the edge of the water.

And the boy held the little sister's hand because they heard again the crash of the waves as they had heard it that night and it seemed to them they could hear too their parents crying out to them from the inflatable boat.

'You know what I'm going to do now,' said the fire. It moved upon the waters. The air grew turbulent around the fire. A hot wind rose and beat back the waves. It beat them to the West and to the East until a great road appeared reaching into the sea. And the fire dried the sand so that it was firm under their feet. And they walked into the sea, with curtains of water on either side of them. They were afraid the sea might overwhelm them but they walked in anyway.

And the boy looked back. He was afraid armoured vehicles would try to follow them. He was afraid that the waters would close over their pursuers.

But this is not what happened.

Ahead of them, the curtains of water drew back a little. Through them stepped many men and many women and many children. A great crowd. And the crowd walked towards the boy and he knew who they were. They were the ones who had been lost in the waters during the days when God had forsaken them.

They were the Lost, who had now become the Found.

And the boy walked towards them.

And the girl walked towards them.

And they knew that the Mother and the Father would be among them.

For the sea would not have them.

And they would walk together and the fire would walk with them, through all the nations of the Earth. Like the Truth.

FICTION

THE OLD STORY

SHERWOOD ANDERSON, 'THE UNTOLD LIE'

Selected by Brian Nellist

Sherwood Anderson (1876–1941), *Winesburg, Ohio* (1919)
'The Untold Lie'

This collection of stories about small town America is dedicated to his mother who 'awoke in me the hunger to see beneath the surface of lives'. To do something you apparently didn't want to do can release feelings you didn't know you had – but which is the lie?

R ay Pearson and Hal Winters were farm hands employed on a farm three miles north of Winesburg. On Saturday afternoons they came into town and wandered about through the streets with other fellows from the country. Ray was a quiet, rather nervous man of perhaps fifty with a brown beard and shoulders rounded by too much and too hard labor. In his nature he was as unlike Hal Winters as two men can be unlike.

Ray was an altogether serious man and had a little sharp-featured wife who had also a sharp voice. The two, with half a dozen thin-legged children, lived in a tumble-down frame house beside a creek at the back end of the Wills farm where Ray was employed.

Hal Winters, his fellow employee, was a young fellow. He was not of the Ned Winters family, who were very respectable people in Winesburg, but was one of the three sons of the old man called Windpeter Winters who had a sawmill near Unionville, six miles away, and who was looked upon by everyone in Winesburg as a confirmed old reprobate.

People from the part of Northern Ohio in which Winesburg lies will remember old Windpeter by his unusual and tragic death. He got drunk one evening in town and started to drive home to Unionville along the railroad tracks. Henry Brattenburg, the butcher, who lived out that way, stopped him at the edge of the town and told him he was sure to meet the down train but Windpeter slashed at him with his whip and drove on. When the train struck and killed him and his two horses a farmer and his wife who were driving home along a nearby road saw the accident. They said that old Windpeter stood up on the seat of his wagon, raving and swearing at the onrushing locomotive, and that he fairly screamed with delight when the team, maddened by his incessant slashing at them, rushed straight ahead to certain death. Boys like young George Willard and Seth Richmond will remember the incident quite vividly because, although everyone in our town said that the old man would go straight to hell and that the community was better off without him, they had a secret conviction that he knew what he was doing and admired his foolish courage. Most boys have seasons of wishing they could die gloriously instead of just being grocery clerks and going on with their humdrum lives.

But this is not the story of Windpeter Winters nor yet of his son Hal who worked on the Wills farm with Ray Pearson. It is Ray's story. It will, however, be necessary to talk a little of young Hal so that you will get into the spirit of it.

Hal was a bad one. Everyone said that. There were three of the Winters boys in that family, John, Hal, and Edward, all broad-shouldered big fellows like old Windpeter himself and all fighters and woman-chasers and generally all-around bad ones.

Hal was the worst of the lot and always up to some devilment.

He once stole a load of boards from his father's mill and sold them in Winesburg. With the money he bought himself a suit of cheap, flashy clothes. Then he got drunk and when his father came raving into town to find him, they met and fought with their fists on Main Street and were arrested and put into jail together.

Hal went to work on the Wills farm because there was a country school teacher out that way who had taken his fancy. He was only twenty-two then but had already been in two or three of what were spoken of in Winesburg as 'women scrapes.' Everyone who heard of his infatuation for the school teacher was sure it would turn out badly. 'He'll only get her into trouble, you'll see,' was the word that went around.

And so these two men, Ray and Hal, were at work in a field on a day in the late October. They were husking corn and occasionally something was said and they laughed. Then came silence. Ray, who was the more sensitive and always minded things more, had chapped hands and they hurt. He put them into his coat pockets and looked away across the fields. He was in a sad, distracted mood and was affected by the beauty of the country. If you knew the Winesburg country in the fall and how the low hills are all splashed with yellows and reds you would understand his feeling. He began to think of the time, long ago when he was a young fellow living with his father, then a baker in Winesburg, and how on such days he had wandered away into the woods to gather nuts, hunt rabbits, or just to loaf about and smoke his pipe. His marriage had come about through one of his days of wandering. He had induced a girl who waited on trade in his father's shop to go with him and something had happened. He was thinking of that afternoon and how it had affected his whole life when a spirit of protest awoke in him. He had forgotten about Hal and muttered words. 'Tricked by Gad, that's what I was, tricked by life and made a fool of,' he said in a low voice.

As though understanding his thoughts, Hal Winters spoke up. 'Well, has it been worth while? What about it, eh? What about marriage and all that?' he asked and then laughed. Hal tried to keep on laughing but he too was in an earnest mood. He began to talk earnestly. 'Has a fellow got to do it?' he asked. 'Has he got to be harnessed up and driven through life like a horse?'

Hal didn't wait for an answer but sprang to his feet and began to walk back and forth between the corn shocks. He was getting more and more excited. Bending down suddenly he picked up an ear of the yellow corn and threw it at the fence. 'I've got Nell Gunther in trouble,' he said. 'I'm telling you, but you keep your mouth shut.'

Ray Pearson arose and stood staring. He was almost a foot shorter than Hal, and when the younger man came and put his two hands on the older man's shoulders they made a picture. There they stood in the big empty field with the quiet corn shocks standing in rows behind them and the red and yellow hills in the distance, and from being just two indifferent workmen they had become all alive to each other. Hal sensed it and because that was his way he laughed. 'Well, old daddy,' he said awkwardly, 'come on, advise me. I've got Nell in trouble. Perhaps you've been in the same fix yourself. I know what everyone would say is the right thing to do, but what do you say? Shall I marry and settle down? Shall I put myself into the harness to be worn out like an old horse? You know me, Ray. There can't anyone break me but I can break myself. Shall I do it or shall I tell Nell to go to the devil? Come on, you tell me. Whatever you say, Ray, I'll do.'

Ray couldn't answer. He shook Hal's hands loose and turning walked straight away toward the barn. He was a sensitive man and there were tears in his eyes. He knew there was only one thing to say to Hal Winters, son of old Windpeter Winters, only one thing that all his own training and all the beliefs of the people he knew would approve, but for his life he couldn't say what he knew he should say.

At half-past four that afternoon Ray was puttering about the barnyard when his wife came up the lane along the creek and called him. After the talk with Hal he hadn't returned to the cornfield but worked about the barn. He had already done the evening chores and had seen Hal, dressed and ready for a roistering night in town, come out of the farmhouse and go into the road. Along the path to his own house he trudged behind his wife, looking at the ground and thinking. He couldn't make out what was wrong. Every time he raised his eyes and saw the beauty of the country in the failing light he wanted to do something he had never done before, shout or scream or hit his wife with his fists or something equally unexpected and terrifying. Along the path he went scratching his head and trying to make it out. He looked hard at his wife's back but she seemed all right.

Sherwood Anderson
Winesburg, Ohio

OXFORD WORLD'S CLASSICS

She only wanted him to go into town for groceries and as soon as she had told him what she wanted began to scold. 'You're always puttering,' she said. 'Now I want you to hustle. There isn't anything in the house for supper and you've got to get to town and back in a hurry.'

Ray went into his own house and took an overcoat from a hook back of the door. It was torn about the pockets and the collar was shiny. His wife went into the bedroom and presently came out with a soiled cloth in one hand and three silver dollars in the other. Somewhere in the house a child wept bitterly and a dog that had been sleeping by the stove arose and yawned. Again the wife scolded. 'The children will cry and cry. Why are you always puttering?' she asked.

Ray went out of the house and climbed the fence into a field. It was just growing dark and the scene that lay before him was lovely. All the low hills were washed with color and even the little clusters of bushes in the corners of the fences were alive with beauty. The whole world seemed to Ray Pearson to have become alive with something just as he and Hal had suddenly become alive when they stood in the corn field staring into each other's eyes.

The beauty of the country about Winesburg was too much for Ray on that fall evening. That is all there was to it. He could not stand it. Of a sudden he forgot all about being a quiet old farm hand and throwing off the torn overcoat began to run across the field. As he ran he shouted a protest against his life, against all life, against everything that makes life ugly. 'There was no promise made,' he cried into the empty spaces that lay about him. 'I didn't promise my Minnie anything and Hal hasn't made any promise to Nell. I know he hasn't. She went into the woods with him because she wanted to go. What he wanted she wanted. Why should I pay? Why should Hal pay? Why should anyone pay? I don't want Hal to become old and worn out. I'll tell him. I won't let it go on. I'll catch Hal before he gets to town and I'll tell him.'

Ray ran clumsily and once he stumbled and fell down. 'I must catch Hal and tell him,' he kept thinking, and although his breath came in gasps he kept running harder and harder. As he ran he thought of things that hadn't come into his mind for years—how at the time he married he had planned to go west to his uncle in Portland, Oregon—how he hadn't wanted to be a farm hand, but had thought when he got out West he would go to sea and be a sailor or get a job on a ranch and ride a horse into Western towns, shouting and laughing and waking the people in the houses with his wild cries. Then as he ran he remembered his children and in fancy felt their hands clutching at him. All of his thoughts of himself were involved with the thoughts of Hal and he thought the children were clutching at the younger man also. 'They are the accidents of life, Hal,' he cried. 'They are not mine or yours. I had nothing to do with them.'

Darkness began to spread over the fields as Ray Pearson ran on and on. His breath came in little sobs. When he came to the fence at the edge of the road and confronted Hal Winters, all dressed up and smoking a pipe as he walked jauntily along, he could not have told what he thought or what he wanted.

Ray Pearson lost his nerve and this is really the end of the story of what happened to him. It was almost dark when he got to the fence and he put his hands on the top bar and stood staring. Hal Winters jumped a ditch and coming up close to Ray put his hands into his pockets and laughed. He seemed to have lost his own sense of what had happened in the corn field and when he put up a strong hand and took hold of the lapel of Ray's coat he shook the old man as he might have shaken a dog that had misbehaved.

'You came to tell me, eh?' he said. 'Well, never mind telling me anything. I'm not a coward and I've already made up my mind.' He laughed again and jumped back across the ditch. 'Nell ain't no fool,' he said. 'She didn't ask me to marry her. I want to marry her. I want to settle down and have kids.'

Ray Pearson also laughed. He felt like laughing at himself and all the world.

As the form of Hal Winters disappeared in the dusk that lay over the road that led to Winesburg, he turned and walked slowly back across the fields to where he had left his torn overcoat. As he went some memory of pleasant evenings spent with the thin-legged children in the tumble-down house by the creek must have come into his mind, for he muttered words. 'It's just as well. Whatever I told him would have been a lie,' he said softly, and then his form also disappeared into the darkness of the fields.

POETRY

IAIN BRITTON

lake prophecies

at lake level the colour of the world

suddenly changes | the water sucks

at milk-green weeds | stars dissolve |

into thousands of white pills | autumn's

leafy tonnage flakes overnight | the sun

pokes at my shoulder | i fall

into a cliff's crease | prophecies

break down | barriers collapse | no one

understands why so many languages

want to be heard at the same time

Share Your Love of Reading in 2018

The Reader wants in 2018 to bring the joy and power of literature to more people across the UK by increasing the number of our Shared Reading groups. Why? Because every week we see how Shared Reading improves people's health and well-being, reduces social isolation and strengthens communities. We are looking for passionate volunteers to join our Shared Reading movement and share their love of literature with others.

Volunteering with The Reader is:

Stimulating A chance to read more, read differently and read with others.

Flexible We know your time is precious, so our training works around you. Then you decide where to run your group; maybe your local library, community centre or care home. We want to hear your ideas.

Sociable You'll meet like-minded people; you could even pair up with a friend to run a group.

There are lots of ways you can get involved, whether it's training to run your own group with our flagship **Read to Lead** programme, becoming a **Shared Reading Organiser** to bring Shared Reading to your community, or simply helping to spread the word about our work and impact with your networks.

We would love to hear from you!

Get in touch at www.thereader.org.uk/volunteer/

THE READER ROOM

THE READER ROOM

SHAKESPEARE'S SONNETS
AND THE NATURE OF AUTISM

Elizabeth Bonapace

t's 2017. Summertime, yet the leaves are turning early this year, the copper beech tree at my mum's is starting to shed hand-sized, desert-dry leaves across the grass which lie scattered amongst my son, L's, collection of outdoor plug sockets, sensors and surveillance cameras, which he has just satisfyingly emptied in a big confused heap on the lawn. It's as if the intricacy of nature's final bounty is somehow indistinguishable from the wires and extractor fans that have been parsed and scrutinised and reworked like some sort of Tate electro-sculpture d'arte.

L dances merrily around his creation telling me with increasing gusto that the sensor is a PIR sensor and that he wants to attach it to an alarm system. This would apparently then beep to let us know if indeed our garden was playing host at night to a hedgehog searching for food – probably foraging the cavalier assembly of slugs that arrive unwittingly every year.

This is our life on the front line of autism. It is a life of wires, of progression and quiet revolution – a revolution that has been sparked by teaching L the immersive lexicon and language of Shakespeare. As Baron-Cohen *et al* discovered in their ground-breaking work published in *Developmental Medicine and Child*

Neurology (2001) – autism is 'characteristically associated with an inability to form normal social relationships or normal communication'. As well as a language barrier, Autistic people tend to have difficulty in reading social cues and facial expression which often results in them becoming isolated from society, all potential seemingly locked away.

Just a few short years ago L was turned away from school and I was advised by a well-meaning home-education officer to consider placing him in a special-needs school for disabled children, because he would 'probably always struggle to communicate'.

> Thy gift, thy tables, are within my brain
> Full charactered with lasting memory
> Which shall above that idle rank remain
> Beyond all date, even to eternity.
> (Shakespeare, Sonnet 122)

Shakespeare uses language as a diverse and obscure instrument, which he parsed and re-worked much as L does his electrical gadgetry, and I realised that this radical use of syntax and vocabulary, using nouns as verbs, and variable and contrasting use of prose and verse – what Professor Philip Davis refers to as 'functional shift' – held much parallel to our front line. Shakespeare, it seems, had an 'intuitive understanding of how our brains work' (Davis, *Shakespeare Thinking*, 2006). For L, learning this language has enabled the rigidity of his mind to 'rewire', to adapt and overcome its original predilection, indeed there is much of that in autism, overcoming and adapting. But it is Shakespeare's poetic insight into humanity and emotion that strikes me most of all, and how his work has helped L to understand feelings.

My mind careers back to our first appointment with a clinical psychologist, Dr David, when L was four. Twenty minutes into that appointment L was diagnosed with classic autism. I remember the shabby blue sofa on which we sat, well used I'd imagined by other parents who had, over the years, sunk into it and looked irrecoverably from the same place as I. L had flopped upside down beside me, his head dangling over the seat cushion, his face impassive, no trace of any thought or feeling could be deduced as he eyed the doctor silently, intriguingly. I remember David trying to coax some words out of him, some form of expression by asking L about his interests, about the 'toy' he'd bought with him – a part of a desk fan upon which two Hex-bug toys and a section of hoover had obligingly been blu-tacked. We didn't need any subsequent sessions of diagnosis, there was no hesitancy.

I recall the desert, uncomfortable feeling of loss which struck me with surprising intensity, quickly followed by my unshakable refusal to accept. I argued against diagnosis, convinced that it was somehow flawed as David sat perplexed in his chair having never been questioned so veraciously, and had hitherto only come across parents actively seeking diagnosis, not resisting it.

But for me acceptance foreboded a loss of direction and the regular, predictable path forwards. It felt like a wayward diversion away from the narrow safety of normality, where other families lived. I did not know in that moment how to be, I had never felt so completely adrift. After the diagnosis, I did not hear from the Psychology team again, I was simply mailed an information pack about autism – the words 'lifelong disability' clearly etched in bold on page one.

> How coldly those impediments stand forth,
> Of wealth, of filial fear, law, kindred, fame?
> Love's arms are peace, 'gainst rule, 'gainst sense, 'gainst shame,
> And sweetens in the suff'ring pangs it bears
> The aloes of all forces, shocks and fears.
> (Shakespeare, 'A Lover's Complaint')

Shakespeare aptly describes love in his sonnets as an aloe, bitter but also a healing balm for life's challenges. The love that a mother has for her child is certainly powerful enough to overcome any shock or fear, and it was our aloe in rebuilding a new way forwards. It is our aloe today as I realise just how far we have come since that diagnosis. Beyond all extensions of logic and thought in Shakespeare's work lies an empathy, a perspicacity about the depth of human emotion. In 1668 John Dryden writes of Shakespeare; 'He was the man who of all modern and perhaps ancient poets had the largest and most comprehensive soul'. And it is this gift that transforms words into a form of expression that an autistic mind can associate with, since those with autism, contrary to traditional understanding, feel emotion with great intensity. The plays and sonnets themselves act as projections of these emotions teaching children to read faces, display feeling and represent themselves in new ways – as in the brilliant work of Kelly Hunter and her Heartbeat teaching method, which has greatly inspired me.

L is now 8, and our home-educating journey has reached its end. He started a mainstream primary school two months ago and came home jubilantly today with an 'outstanding' sticker for reading aloud and acting out a fable in front of his class. He has even made a friend called Lewis who likes football, hopping races and now PIR sensors. I experienced my first ever parents' evening last week; the teacher praised L's extraordinary language skills and vocabulary as 'something we can all learn from', but most importantly said that he is happy. She mentioned how his face lights up with laughter as he plays with the other children at playtime, and shares jokes with them. In the first week she said that he was upset and had shed a tear because he was missing me. But then there had been a Science lesson and he forgot his sadness, eagerly telling the class all he knew about Cassini's final fiery plunge into Saturn's midst, how intrigued he is about our Universe, and how he wants to launch a PIR sensor up into space to see what happens, and be the first to detect an image of the black hole at the centre of our Galaxy.

I reflect upon whether it is the refusal to accept the diagnosis and its limitations that has bought us this far, for it was that which drove us towards our Shakespeare revolution. That the autistic mind might be pliable and not rigid as once assumed, and in the right terrain be able to blossom into whatever brilliant future we can envisage, echoing the intricacies of electro art, black holes and the scope and breadth of Shakespeare's words. It is increasingly evident that language and vocabulary skills underpin everything else, especially so the expression of emotion and feeling which rely upon an understanding of how words associate and portend sentiment.

I wonder too if it is love that is the immovable anchor that underlies every success, love which 'looks on tempests and is never shaken, / It is the star to every wand'ring bark, whose worth's unknown' (Shakespeare, Sonnet 116).

Read Elizabeth's first piece on her son on our blog: http://www.blog.thereader.org.uk/

THE READER ROOM

ASK THE READER

Brian Nellist

Q When I think of the bitterness of contemporary political and social controversy I'm surprised by the absence of serious literary satire. Where is today's equivalent of *Animal Farm*, say? On the other hand when I remember with what boredom in the sixth form I was taken through Pope's 'Epistle to Arbuthnot', maybe it's just as well. Reading it became a study of footnotes about historical personages who meant nothing to me and who were remote from my interests. Need satire be always buried in a minutely detailed present that soon becomes an irrelevant past?

A The difficulty has always been felt. It was Swift, I think, who pointed out to Pope that since the figures in the *Dunciad* were attacked for trivialising contemporary thought and discourse, in ten years time they would have been forgotten anyway. But then great satire transforms distinct and recognisable individuals, 'real' people if you like, into images of characteristic human weakness and failings, a kind of static drama. Since you mention it, it's much less important (in the poem to Arbuthnot) that Atticus is a portrait of Addison than who he is made to be in Pope's imagination. Personal quarrels matter less, indeed become insignificant, besides the recognisable character of a flawed human being. Moral perception and convincing psychology matter more than how and why the author turned against his erstwhile associate. The other side of blame is praise but Atticus turns generosity of response into veiled grudge:

> Damn with faint praise, assent with civil leer,
> And without sneering, taught the rest to sneer;
> Willing to wound, and yet afraid to strike,
> Just hint a faint and hesitate dislike...

How easy it is in the face of some great achievement to preserve one's freedom of judgement by minor quibbles when all the time these quibbles disguise envy. Cowardice blunts honest approval and presents itself instead as politeness, 'civil leer'. The actual hostility felt, turned into hints and hesitations, wins a reputation for good nature. If you don't recognise that, certainly in the professional reviews one reads in papers and journals, but most shamingly as at least a possibility in oneself then you're a better man than I am Gunga Din. The portrait has all the complexity of character you would expect to find in a realist novel. With Sporus however, the other sustained character in the poem, we descend into a place of utter corruption. The notes tell us Sporus is a portrait of Lord Harvey, a sexually ambiguous minor politician who switched allegiances, but who now cares? What matters is the image of degradation and evil:

> *Eve*'s tempter thus the Rabbins have exprest,
> A Cherub's face, a reptile all the rest;
> Beauty that shocks you, parts that none will trust,
> Wit that can creep, and pride that licks the dust.

Compared with Atticus there is a kind of honesty in the vileness of Sporus. He is what he seems, untrustworthy, venomous, a failed Satan, 'at the ear of Eve, familiar Toad' in Miltonic terms. The vigour of the verse expresses an honest hatred in the poet himself; 'there then, that's got rid of that'.

And all the time there is another voice at work in the poem. It is a recurrent dialogue with interruptions by John Arbuthnot, Pope's friend and doctor for his lifelong illness who likes to modify the anger for the sake of his patient's health. In a kind of parallel world there are other figures of affection, Swift for example and Gay. From the opening line 'Shut, shut the door' it's as though the whole poem is an attempt to exclude the terrible images projected on the mental screen, to protect the intimacies of personal life. Pope's family was Catholic of course and hence under permanent suspicion. His mother still, but barely, lived at the age of ninety-three and his father had died in 1717, two years after the last Jacobite uprising. After all the false speaking by the figures in the poem he remembers that father's truthfulness:

> Unlearn'd, he knew no schoolman's subtle art,
> No language, but the language of the heart

As always in the poem the apparent haphazard onslaught on the hypocrites and bad-mouthers has been leading up to that wonderful phrase 'the language of the heart'. The translator of Homer for his age salutes the only essential language for all men. In the greatest satire, blame is balanced by praise, by the recognition of values beyond the wearisomeness and mess of misbehaviour, somehow to get from the scornful public voice to the warmth of the private. Too much of our contemporary work in the genre sacrifices everything to laughter without the grandeur that Pope and Johnson and Dryden achieve and without any sense of the human values that are being betrayed.

THE READER ROOM

BLANKS

Grace Farrington

think it may be quite a common experience to feel surprise upon re-reading an earlier piece of writing, in one's own hand. For me the surprise is one of reassurance: that there is actually something there. It marks the fact that I was in some way present at another time, and that I was able to get something out back then, in fact sometimes more than I would now have expected.

Without this written testimony, I live in fear of the blank, the possibility that I have nothing to say, or that there is a nothing where I want to be able to offer a something. It is a realistic fear, too, because quite often I have been caught out by my own mind at those moments where I most want to be able to rely on it. The first memory I have of this really mattering was in a written exam at school. There was a particular exam, and I don't remember what the subject was, but I do remember the occasion of sitting in the hall, conscious that time was of the essence, and that every moment counted, and yet unable for some small window to get into gear, regardless of what the questions were or what might have been required of me. What comes next? What can possibly come next when you have nothing?

In more recent years this has tended to happen most frequently during conversations, where I am face to face with someone. To my great frustration, it happened rather memorably when I interviewed for a place on an undergraduate degree course. Whilst studying for my English A-level, I had fallen into what I now remember as a pretty consuming and passionate love-affair with literature, which I have not felt quite in the same way or to the same degree either before or since. It seemed terribly unfair therefore when it came to the crunch point and I was asked what I was studying by a person of what I viewed as eminence and could barely even recall the titles of the books.

But exams and interviews are rather heightened forms of ordinary life and I care more about the ordinary in the end. It wouldn't be so bad if the blanks only came during moments of intensity or pressure. Instead, it feels like they are always a lurking threat, a fault of a temperamental wiring system that can stay connected for quite extended periods of time, but always carries the risk of cutting out, leaving those I am talking to hanging for an answer. Regardless of how this feels though as a problem to have, in reality I cannot afford to allow it to be a problem, and so I have tried to get better at mopping up my thoughts and presenting some sort of response, whether it be verbal or non-verbal. It has taken some time for me to painfully learn that this is up to me, and that I cannot hope to be rescued in such situations, especially when talking with people with whom there is no particular personal relationship to fall back on.

It interests me, then, when I am faced with a blank in another person, which on reflection has been quite a regular part of my experience in Shared Reading with others within settings based not only in the community, but also in care homes and mental health inpatient services. This is hard to deal with, and quite often unsettling. From what I have noticed of myself and others, the way in which one responds as a result can either be *with* the difficulty, making an effort to partner with it, or *against* it. Here too, one's own fear and discomfort again come into play.

Recently, I've been reading with several older people in a service that supports those living with dementia in the local community. One of the challenges has been that with a couple of the group members, regardless of their feeling about poetry, I have the impression that they have become unused to being engaged in conversation, or being called upon to say something about what is going on for them. One woman comes with her carer, who is diligent, patient and practical, and speaks about the range of meals that she thoughtfully prepares back at home, knowing the tastes of the person she is assisting. But there is not quite a natural bond between the two, and without any prompt or stimulation being present, they tend to fall silent alongside one another. The one man in the group comes without his wife. He is rather taciturn, an effect it seems of the frustration he must feel at not knowing why he is there, as well as a more persistent low mood that for him has begun to accompany his increasing symptoms of dementia.

The last thing I want to do is to leave these people in the condition of silence, because it doesn't feel as though anything is happening there, and I am interested rather in where the alive part of these people might be, since I do believe this exists somewhere, however hidden or buried. But I also don't want to presume upon people's feelings, understanding or willingness to engage: to make any assumptions feels too risky here. What I realise at this stage is that I don't know exactly what to do, or how successful my efforts are going to be. What I am sure of is that I am going to have to feel my way, and do my best to open up the poems to the group in the hope that this will in turn give the group members as many op-portunities as possible to do likewise, to feel that opening within themselves.

Initially I read the whole of the poem by Mary Oliver, 'When I Am Among the Trees', and begin to talk a little about going among trees, before going back to re-read the first verse:

> When I am among the trees,
> especially the willows and the honey locust,
> equally the beech, the oaks and the pines,
> they give off such hints of gladness.
> I would almost say that they save me, and daily.

I am not completely sure why these particular trees are listed, especially given the willow's traditional association with weeping. But the bit that I do feel I can hang onto in this verse is those 'hints of gladness'. It is a lovely phrase and I like the fact that these are 'hints' rather than anything bolder or bigger. Is it a kind of suggestion, and is this about the gladness of the tree itself or a suggestion of a gladness that the tree might pass on? I don't ask these questions but I do ask what people make of this phrase, and whether they've ever felt something similar. There is a pause, and then one of the staff members in the group begins to talk about the trees she recalls from her own home country, bearing exotic fruit such as the coconut. Hints of gladness begin to come through here, both via that memory of home, and a very different landscape, but also through the pleasure that the discovery of such fruit could bring, back then. She smiles as she speaks, and suddenly the other staff seem to recognise too that there is a clue here to unlocking the experience of some of the group members. When Zed is asked about the kinds of trees he remembers from Jamaica, he gives a wry smile and tells us about the plentiful mangos which formed such a regular part of life on the island. I suspect the hints of gladness were reflected on our own faces here as we listened to him and tried to imagine for ourselves what it would have been like for him growing up in such a rich natural environment.

We spend most of the session on the poem, and find some genuine thoughts arising from it, at least once from a group member, and also in a number of instances from the staff members. I am struck however, after the session, by how Zed is still sat there next to me looking over the copies, running his finger along some of the lines of one of the poems, trying to make out the words. I wonder at this point if he can read, but then I also remember hearing that he liked reading. Perhaps it is getting harder for him to decipher different words, or to link them to their individual meanings? Could there be any words here that he has never come across before? This makes me reflect on where Zed was at when we were trying to read and talk about the poems earlier, and question whether the poem in and of itself meant anything to him at that stage. I feel that in a way this is the starting point that we have been trying to get to, and it feels a shame that I cannot simply start again with Zed there and then.

I wonder if the task of the group leader in such circumstances is to read into the blank, to try and ascertain where it comes from or what might be behind it. I am thinking of a child who lacks confidence in reading, where the barrier might be a combination of a habitual switching off to activities at which the child believes they are no good, coupled with that lack of practice and positive reinforcement which means that it feels even harder to initiate a response. In another group, it might be a woman who enjoys coming along each week, and finds that making this regular commitment is useful in helping her to manage her depression, but who never responds to questions in the group as if they might have been addressed to her, or as if she might have an answer to contribute in response to them. It is like there has been an opting-out, but one is not even conscious of having decided to do so, or it has been like this for so long that one cannot remember when or how it started.

In a filmed session where the group meets in a library, there is one woman who is very much part of the group, but who actually says little. She initially met the group leader in an inpatient setting for people with learning disabilities, but since her discharge from the unit, Anne has made the significant step of continuing on with the reading group by joining one that the group leader runs in the community. To start with she was accompanied to the group by a support worker, who helped Anne out with navigating local public transport links, but more recently, Anne has made the journey on her own. The group leader is understandably pleased and somewhat proud of Anne for sticking at it, and for sticking with her too, in this way.

Anne sits next to the group leader, and unlike Zed is keen to engage, making some considerable effort to follow along and play her part. As the first few paragraphs of the story are read aloud and considered, Anne keeps shifting backwards and forwards in the chair, leaning into the story and back out again, as she looks at the page and then looks up at times, smiling in response to certain comments made by other group members. She too follows the reading of the lines with her finger, showing care and concentration. Yet there are limits to Anne's contributions. She enjoys having a go at reading aloud, and is the first to do so after the group leader, but when it comes to it she is neither clear enough nor loud enough for others to hear what is being read, though the group accommodate this with patience and ease as the other members follow along using their own copies. Anne is also unlikely to answer questions posed by the group leader, except with a simple 'yes' of agreement, which now and again does feel like her way of joining in.

The group leader is warm and inclusive, turning to Anne at times and smiling at her as she looks around the group. But the only time when she actually addresses Anne directly is in response to a line in the story about the protagonist's view of life. Della, despite her very best efforts at saving and bartering, has finally accepted that the amount of money she is going to be able to spend on a Christmas present for her husband is pitifully meagre.

> There was clearly nothing to do but flop down on the shabby little couch and howl. So Della did it. Which instigates the moral reflection that life is made up of sobs, sniffles, and smiles, with sniffles predominating.
> 'The Gift of the Magi', O. Henry

It is a casual little sentence, one that does not particularly get to the heart of such hardship, but it has its point and my own instinct here would be that it is a natural conclusion for someone to come to in such a situation. It feels important for the story that as readers we can identify with Della in this. But in order to probe this idea, the group leader in the session re-reads the sentence with some surprise in her voice, and asks Anne: 'do sniffles predominate in your life, or do smiles predominate?' Anne, laughing in response, replies: 'smiles'. On first viewing of the video, I had thought this rather beside the point. But on reflection, I started to notice of Anne that actually her way of communicating, when she was not looking around wide-eyed and unsure of herself, was in fact through smiles. What she represented in the group was neither the interpreter of meaning, nor the person who brings their own lively anecdotes to the reading, nor even the person who offers quiet little nuggets of insight when these feel least expected. Rather, Anne had her own role as the keen smiler, and a companionable presence next to the other quiet female in the group.

So where, then, does this leave us in relation to the challenge of the blank? For these examples could not really be called wow moments, and neither does it feel like this is the direction in which we are necessarily heading with these individuals. But if Shared Reading is not to be only for the few, there has to be an attempt to help group members to find a way in, wherever they might be starting from. This is one little version of that attempt, and I hope this might just help open our eyes to many more.

MEDICS ARE HUMAN!

Jane Davis

've just finished Sam Guglani's *Histories*.

Medics are human!

So hard to remember this when they are speaking to you as though you aren't, or when, godlike, they are fixing you.

Hard for the medics, too, when much of their training and daily grind conspire to create a wall of (sometimes vital) professionalism between them and us.

When my father-in-law had cancer we did not care one jot about the human skills of the consultant: we just wanted Big Science to come with its battering rams and attack the disease. Later, we were touched by the kindness of the man whose medicine could not save the day, but whose shared humanity lit Dad's last weeks with loving concern. That loving concern, the exchange of feeling between doctor and patient, human and human, is Sam Guglani's subject matter, both in this novel and his extra-curricular activities as an oncologist in Cheltenham, and the founder of Medicine Unboxed, which aims to engage health professionals and the public in conversation around medicine, illuminated through the arts (www.medicineunboxed.org).

I saw Sam speak a couple of weeks ago at Gladstone's Library, partly a reading from the book, partly a talk about the need for medicine and art to meet, particularly literature, more often, and more publicly. As he spoke I remembered some work I'd done with medical students when we had a few years' experiment with literature modules in the School of Medicine at Liverpool – first, how hard those medical students were willing to work, something some arts students might have profitably learned from. Second, how useful some of them found poetry. Third how distressing some members of some Shared Reading groups found it to have a student doctor in their midst – as if the enemy had shown up in your sanctuary.

It seemed to me that Sam Guglani might help spearhead a movement to change that dynamic, and I was a bit sorry that he was an oncologist: we need him to work in mental health.

Of course, there are many humane, careful, loving people working in the discipline of psychiatry. I know some of them. But not many people I meet through Shared Reading seem to have been in relation to them in many years engagement with Mental Health Services. Hence the distress of some group members when finding 'doctors' on placement in Shared Reading groups some years ago.

After he'd finished speaking, Sam read the opening chapter of the novel, which made a great stand alone story, strangely shocking.

I bought the book and read it last week – a set of inter-related stories from hospital; doctors, patients, cleaners, nurses, porters, doctors-as-patients, the voices are woven into a swelling chorale. This is human life in a contemporary hospital, a workplace, the demands of being human often pressured out of kilter by the demands of ordinary organisational any-workplace situations. Anyone at work can find the printer's broken, the IT help-desk not helpful, I haven't managed to grab any lunch, am worried about home, or am still flustered by what happened before… but here, you are face to face with the next patient, and another test of your often failing humanity:

> They're waiting, someone is always waiting, always wanting something from her, wanting an answer. Even

now, looking away from both of them and down at the notes on her lap, Emily feels the couple sitting there tight-lipped and straight-backed, the entitled press of their stares.

She's been falling in slow motion from the minute she walked in here, apologising but not really meaning it. No, she had meant it, she was sorry, but only just. In a contest of apologies it would be weightless: sorry to keep you waiting, sorry, you've months to live; sorry, these days I struggle to feel very much for you, my patients.

She'd sat next door first, hoping to read through the notes and print off a path report. But the printer had crashed again, its red light blinking after brief, hopeful whirrs. She called IT and someone young, some terribly young and relaxed-sounding girl, said it was too late in the day, that they couldn't possibly fix it now, surely there must be another printer? Then Nancy had arrived, telling her that Freda, their woman on the ward, was set to leave, she wouldn't stay in for tomorrow's MRI, that her daughter and husband were with her and they were packing up. This news, this and the sound of the clicking printer, pushed Emily from her chair and propelled her into the consultation, unprepared and flustered.

It's little moments like that, almost unspottable, that make Sam Guglani such an excellent human diagnostician. That the printer could have pushed you, that the previous patient's walking out could have propelled you into action with the next patient, like a domino fall, one into the other, with your conscious self scrabbling about behind, trying to self-question. Am I sorry? No? Yes? A bit? He is carefully observing and describing humans asked to work in overly demanding and finally inhumane situations, mostly doing their failing best.

Guglani wants to draw attention to the failings as well as the best efforts. He's angry, often through the non-medical voices in the book, the porter, the hairdresser, or here, the medical secretary:

Take Munro in our office yesterday, telling us all about Jim. I've some bad news everyone, he says. And even then his voice stays hollow. How must that be for a patient? Important words offered as empy sound. I stood at the back of the room and watched him as he talked at us.

'Important words offered as empty sound… he talked at us' Of course we all get angry about this, and it is us non-medics perhaps who feel it most. But this isn't a critique to be applied only to senior doctors. I've met it often in professional, highly educated people, women as well as men, who use it as cover, a kind of armour. As members of a civil society, we have to ask ourselves, why do such people need that armour?

For the medics, the pressure to save lives, to heal, to offer cure is a hard pressure to bear for the best among us. For more on that read John Berger's *A Forunate Man*. *Histories* would also sit well with a rereading of Lydgate's part in *Middlemarch*. I feel a weekend study group on medics and literature coming on…

With this novel Sam Guglani joins a fine tradition of doctor-writers – he quoted Chekov (much read in Shared Reading groups) at the start of his talk, and I thought as he spoke about William Carlos Williams and Oliver Sacks. I remembered, too, the group of medical students I spent an afternoon with who berated me for thinking they had time to waste on literature – we have blood clots and heart attacks to learn about! People could die!

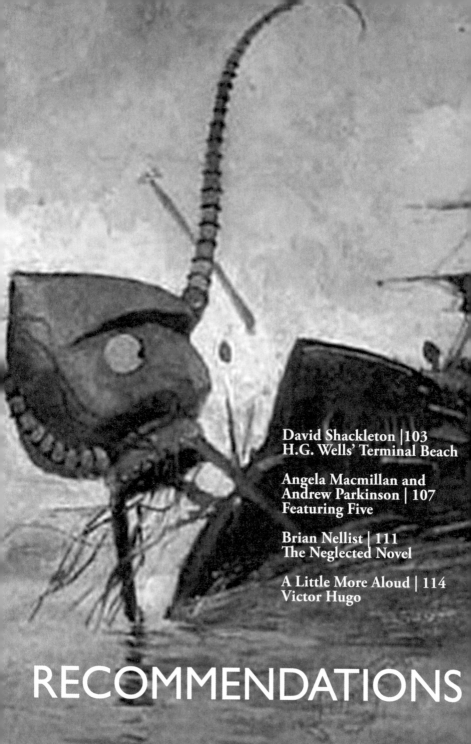

RECOMMENDATIONS

Henrique Alvim Corrêa illustration for 1906 edition HG Wells' *The War Of The Worlds*

RECOMMENDATIONS

H.G. WELLS'S TERMINAL BEACH

David Shackleton

Towards the end of H.G. Wells's *The Time Machine*, the Time Traveller boards his machine and plunges 'into futurity'. That which confronts him is awful, and yet he feels compelled to keep watching. He slows down his machine 'until the dim outlines of a desolate beach grew visible'.

In imagining this journey, Wells drew on the romantic poetry which so inspired him as a young man. For instance, the 'rayless obscurity' of Wells's scene echoes Byron's poem 'Darkness' (1816), in which the poet dreams that 'The bright sun was extinguish'd, and the stars/ Did wander darkling in the eternal space,/ Rayless, and pathless, and the icy earth/ Swung blind and blackening in the moonless air'. Yet just as important as any literary influence is the science that Wells studied at the Normal School of Science.

Wells did not come from a wealthy background: his mother was a housekeeper, and at fourteen he became an apprentice to a draper. Nevertheless, he benefitted from the Education Act of 1870, and won a scholarship to study at the Normal School of Science in London. It was there that he studied biology under the charismatic T.H. Huxley, who is today remembered as 'Darwin's bulldog'. Wells later described the year that he spent in Huxley's class as unquestionably the most educational year in his life. His study of science fuelled his imagination, and fed into his early scientific romances, which include *The Time Machine*, *The Island of Doctor Moreau*, and *The War of the Worlds*.

The future envisaged in *The Time Machine* is one shaped by nineteenth-century science. (Indeed, Wells sent a copy of his book to Huxley, with a letter saying that its central idea was the result of a certain amount of biological study). Geologists such as Charles Lyell had sought to reconstruct the geohistory of the earth, claiming that it was immensely older than many supposed. Charles Darwin's theory of evolution by natural selection suggested that humans had evolved slowly from other forms of life over a vast period of time, and were susceptible to evolve further in the future in the form of either a biological progression or a retrogression. Physical theorists such as William Thomson argued that the earth was younger than geologists claimed, and (in accordance with the second law of thermodynamics) that it was undergoing a physical decay through the dissipation of mechanical energy. *The Time Machine* combines the vastly extended time-scale of the geologists, with an evolutionary scenario in which humanity has degenerated into distinct species, and a thermodynamic scenario in which the earth suffers a heat-death.

The terminal beach is the culmination of these scientific scenarios. Humans appear to have fallen extinct. Certainly, the Traveller finds no easily-recognisable descendants of humans — not even the degenerate Eloi and Morlocks of the year 802,701 A.D. Instead, he encounters a 'thing like a huge white butterfly' and monstrous 'crab-like' creatures; travelling further into the future, even this 'crawling multitude of crabs' has disappeared, and the beach appears 'lifeless'. The physical effects brought about by the thermodynamic dissipation of energy are similarly nightmarish, as the Traveller finds himself on a frozen beach assailed by a 'bitter cold'. He watches 'the life of the old earth ebb away' with a 'strange fascination' that turns to horror. He describes how a 'horror of this great darkness came on me', and of how in the 'rayless obscurity' he was struck by a 'terrible dread of lying helpless in that remote and awful twilight'. His experience is described using the lexicon of the sublime: 'obscurity', 'horror', 'terrible', 'dread', 'awful'.

Roger Luckhurst has identified Wells's beach scene as one possible origin of science fiction as a genre, and suggests that it helped to invent the 'cosmic sublime' of science fiction that was later developed by writers such as Arthur Clarke and Isaac Asimov. While Luckhurst credits Wells with the creation of what was to become the 'science fiction sublime', this aesthetic can be traced back to geological literature.

Geologists frequently deployed an aesthetic of wonder, whereby the immensity of geological time could bewilder the mind into a temporary and pleasurable loss of rationality. For example, John Playfair famously described listening to the eminent geologist James Hutton lecturing on the rocks at Siccar Point as an experience in which the 'mind seemed to grow giddy by looking so far into the abyss of time'. Although Wells's Traveller voyages literally rather than imaginatively, and into the future rather than into the past, the sublimity of his journey is heir to such an aesthetic of the sublime.

Standing on the desolate beach in the distant future, the Traveller grows 'giddy'. This giddiness is most immediately explained by the disorienting rocking of his machine, and the thinness of the air of the future, yet it also echoes Playfair's description of the extremity of his imaginative voyage back through time. In an earlier version of *The Time Machine*, the Traveller had described his planned journey into the extreme future in terms which again echo Playfair: 'I resolved to run on for one glimpse of the still remoter future — one peep into the deeper abysm of time — and then to return to you and my own epoch'. Playfair's 'abyss of time' becomes Wells's 'abysm of time', and his visual metaphor of 'looking' becomes Wells's 'glimpse' and 'peep'. The Time Traveller's terminus, at which he grows giddy and needs to return, is both the extreme point to which he can travel into a world which is increasingly unable to support life, and also parallels the limit at which the imagination becomes overwhelmed in a sublime confrontation with deep time, before needing to return to the present day.

ONE PAGER

" So I travelled, stopping ever and again, in great strides of a thousand years or more, drawn on by the mystery of the earth's fate, watching with a strange fascination the sun grow larger and duller in the westward sky, and the life of the old earth ebb away. At last, more than thirty million years hence, the huge red-hot dome of the sun had come to obscure nearly a tenth part of the darkling heavens. Then I stopped once more... and the red beach, save for its livid green liverworts and lichens, seemed lifeless. And now it was flecked with white. A bitter cold assailed me. Rare white flakes ever and again came eddying down. ... There were fringes of ice along the sea margin, with drifting masses further out; but the main expanse of that salt ocean, all bloody under the eternal sunset, was still unfrozen. ...

The darkness grew apace; a cold wind began to blow in freshening gusts from the east, and the showering white flakes in the air increased in number. From the edge of the sea came a ripple and whisper. Beyond these lifeless sounds the world was silent. Silent? It would be hard to convey the stillness of it. All the sounds of man, the bleating of sheep, the cries of birds, the hum of insects, the stir that makes the background of our lives — all that was over. ... At last, one by one, swiftly, one after the other, the white peaks of the distant hills vanished into blackness. ... I saw the black central shadow of the eclipse sweeping towards me. In another moment the pale stars alone were visible. All else was rayless obscurity. The sky was absolutely black.

A horror of this great darkness came on me. The cold, that smote to my marrow, and the pain I felt in breathing, overcame me. ... I got off the machine to recover myself. I felt giddy and incapable of facing the return journey. ... Then I felt I was fainting. But a terrible dread of lying helpless in that remote and awful twilight sustained me while I clambered upon the saddle.'

The Terminal Beach, from H. G. Wells's *The Time Machine* (1895)

RECOMMENDATIONS

FEATURING FIVE

Angela Macmillan and Andrew Parkinson

Anthony Trollope, *The Eustace Diamonds* (1871)
OUP ISBN-13: 978-0199587780

This is the third in the Palliser series but it's entirely possible to read it as a stand alone novel. 'It was admitted by all her friends, and also by her enemies – who were in truth the more numerous and active body of the two – that Lizzie Greystock had done very well with herself.' Lizzie's wealthy husband dies before the story opens leaving her with a son, a castle and The Eustace Diamonds. However, it seems that Lizzie is not legally entitled to the diamonds and must give them up. This she has no intention of doing. Her full intention of finding another husband involves her cousin Frank; a lord and politician; a disreputable aristocrat and a vulgar clergyman and all become immersed in a confusion of politics, moral dishonesty, legal argument and actual crime. With every chapter Trollope gradually tightens his grip so that Frank and Lizzie slowly accommodate themselves to their wrongdoing, hardly noticing it in their ongoing everyday lives. It's fascinating to watch.

Helen Hull, *Heat Lightning* (1931)
Persephone ISBN-13: 978-1903155912

As this very good novel opens we find Amy Norton at the start of a week's visit to her family home in Michigan. It is ten months since the Wall Street Crash and the family firm is suffering. Unknown to her parents, Amy's marriage is in trouble and she had hoped to find some respite away from New York. But events intervene and she is forced to view her family objectively; to think of them as separate people, not just aunts, cousins, grandmothers etc. Consequently she begins to understand more about herself as a woman and in relationship: 'She was beginning to think, instead of moving round in a treadmill of emotional catchwords.' Helen Hull is hugely perceptive about the way we interact with our families, patterns of behavior and the workings of marriage. It is set in a time of change in America but mostly it's about the possibility of a discovery of personal values to hold onto in times of change – a code for life.

Sebastian Barry, *Days Without End* (2016)
Faber ISBN-13: 978-0571277049

The relentless violence in this novel makes it difficult to read. What saves it is the surprising tenderness. Barry's writing combines realism with nightmare in the affecting life story of Thomas McNulty who first escapes The Great Famine in Ireland and, still a child of fourteen, makes the appalling journey by sea to America. He arrives ill and destitute but meets up with John Cole, a boy of similar background and together these two 'wood-shavings of humanity in a rough world' find work as dance partners to lonely men in a mining town. When they can no longer pass as girls, they take the only option open to them and enlist in the US Army to fight in the Indian Wars and later the American Civil War. The boys loved each other at first sight and eventually become lovers without knowing any names or precedent for what they are. Against a background of shocking brutality, they simply love each other and this is what gives life meaning and purpose. "How we were able to see slaughter without flinching. Because we were nothing ourselves, to begin with". The path from nothing to something is the hope the book hangs on.

Amy Liptrot, *The Outrun* (2016)
Canongate ISBN-13: 978-1782115489

This memoir is a testament to the possibility of recovery. Amy Liptrot tells of her desire to escape the confined life of Orkney where her farmer father is bi-polar and her mother a born-again Christian. Once she gets to London her life increasingly revolves around drinking and Amy is unsparing in her descriptions of debasement and destructive alcoholism. Eventually she enters a community detox programme and against all odds gets through. 'Coming out of rehab was not the end of the story but the beginning… staying sober is a daily challenge'. In order to face it she decides, at the age of thirty, to go home. Back in The Orkneys, it is as if she exchanges an obsession with drink for an obsession with the natural world around her. With an energy that suffuses the book she attunes her inner self to the outer space of the islands to their history and wildlife, to the seas and to the stars, and begins, remarkably, to restore, in an odd combination of strength and fragility, a sense of reconnection.

Ra Page, editor, *Protest: Stories of Resistance* (2017)
Comma Press ISBN-13: 978-1905583737

Protest is a powerful collection of short stories which illustrates the human struggles encapsulated within various protest movements throughout British history. Uprisings range from The Peasants' Revolt of 1381 to the demonstrations against the Iraq war in 2003, with stories from *The Reader* magazine regulars Frank Cottrell-Boyce (A Fiery Flag Unfurled in Coleman Street) and David Constantine (Rivers of Blood).

The collection argues that the current socio-political climate we live in is far from an anomaly, but the failure to learn from the follies of history; a vindication of George Santayana's declaration that 'those who cannot remember the past are condemned to repeat it'. Protest illuminates the bravery of dissenting voices and challenges the reader to place themselves at the right side of history in these turbulent and uncertain times.

(Andrew Parkinson)

Edited by
ANGELA MACMILLAN

A Little,
ALOUD
with Love

Prose and poetry for
reading aloud to someone
you love

RECOMMENDATIONS

THE NEGLECTED NOVEL

CHARLES DICKENS, 'GEORGE SILVERMAN'S EXPLANATION'

Brian Nellist

Charles Dickens (1812–70), 'George Silverman's Explanation' (1868), *Reprinted Pieces* **(1874)**

This is not a novel, scarcely a novella, yet in nine chapters it is longer than a short story, and it is Dickens' last completed narrative. Looking around I find few friends have read it and indeed it is a very strange work. An elderly clergyman tells his life story but he is so lacking in self-confidence that having begun with half a sentence he breaks off two very short chapters until in the third he tries to find 'the natural manner'. His whole life is an attempt to overcome the effects of a destructive childhood worse than that of Pip in *Great Expectations*. He was born in a cellar in Preston into penury and filth, neglected by parents who are dirt poor; scarcely clothed, scarcely fed, never seeing the light of day, resented by his mother for having needs and called by her 'a worldly little devil', since she had been brought up in some extreme sect. When they die of the fever he is eventually discovered starving and brought up to be fumigated in the street. All he can say is 'I am hungry and thirsty'. A ring of people stand and stare at this creature; 'I knew at the time they had a horror of me but I couldn't help it'. His Birmingham grandfather who had property has also just died, and Mr Hawkyard, a preacher, turns up to collect the child who, because it was his mother's single boast, asks 'where's his houses?'

> 'Hah! Horrible worldliness on the edge of the grave' said
> Mr Hawkyard, casting more of the vinegar over me, as if
> to get the devil out of me.

What is to happen to such children is the question Dickens asks many times, in *Bleak House* with Jo, in the Christmas writings, but the answer here is surprising. Brother Hawkyard takes responsibility, after purloining the grandfather's property, and places George in a school attached to the ruin of Hoghton Tower, a sixteenth-century large house still there not far from Preston and the boy turns out to be intelligent and teachable. So wounded, however, by his infant horrors that with a kind of induced autism he can relate to no other human being. All that matters with him is his books which demand nothing of him. Yet though he cannot respond to the girl from the neighbouring farmhouse who takes pity on him, 'this holding her in my thoughts' at least helps 'to the humanising of myself'. His scholarly abilities however win him a place at a Cambridge College, much to the disgust of Hawkyard and co. who see it as a sign of the never to be overcome 'worldliness'. 'Are the angels learned?' he asks, 'They don't so much as know their alphabet'.

At university he is again solitary yet he can explain the ideas in the books he reads and survives by becoming a coach to less able students. The story is I suppose another of Dickens' answers to what might have happened had he never really escaped the blacking factory. The mother of one of his pupils Lady Fareway offers him a very small benefice, a parish in remotest Devon, so long as he becomes her unpaid secretary and tutors her daughter Adelina who can't of course enter higher education though George finds her a more gifted pupil than her brother. This is a tale of apparently stifled lives that still overcome their hazards. You'll see what happens; they fall in love. Yet so great is Silverman's sense of shame that of course he cannot accept it. Instead he helps her to love another pupil by giving him his own tastes and ideas;

> I made my tuition less imaginative than before; separated myself from my poets and philosophers; careful to present them in their own lives and me, the lonely servant, in my own shade.

There is so much hypocrisy surrounding him in the tale one is tempted to doubt his account but that temptation is to be resisted or the story loses its point. The world judges by what it knows and the utter annihilation of self, not in itself a good thing, is interpreted simply as a more devious kind of personal interest by Lady Fareway. There is at least a bitterness when he surrenders Adelina which confirms his sense of loss as he marries the two students;

> To send them forth husband and wife into the shining world with golden gates that awaited them.

Yes, they stand by him along with other supporters and the story ends with a kind of peace but no wonder Dickens himself thought it was a strange tale to come uninvited into his mind.

A LITTLE MORE ALOUD

VICTOR HUGO

LES MISERABLES

Selected by Angela Macmillan

Volume I, Book Fifth, Chapter VI

After 19 years in the prison Bagne of Toulon for the crime of stealing bread for his starving sister, Jean Valjean has come to Montreuil-sur-Mer where, using the name Monsieur Madeleine, he has become in time a wealthy factory owner and eventually the town mayor. Unfortunately the new police inspector, Javert, was formerly a guard at Bagne of Toulon and is already suspicious of Madeleine's true identity.

One morning M. Madeleine was passing through an unpaved alley of M. sur M.; he heard a noise, and saw a group some distance away. He approached. An old man named Father Fauchelevent had just fallen beneath his cart, his horse having tumbled down.

This Fauchelevent was one of the few enemies whom M. Madeleine had at that time. When Madeleine arrived in the neighborhood, Fauchelevent, an ex-notary and a peasant who was almost educated, had a business which was beginning to be in a bad way. Fauchelevent had seen this simple workman grow rich, while he, a lawyer, was being ruined. This had filled him with jealousy, and he had done all he could, on every occasion, to injure Madeleine. Then bankruptcy had come; and as the old man had nothing left but a cart and a horse, and neither family nor children, he had turned carter.

The horse had two broken legs and could not rise. The old man was caught in the wheels. The fall had been so unlucky that the whole weight of the vehicle rested on his breast. The cart was quite heavily laden. Father Fauchelevent was rattling in the throat in the most lamentable manner. They had tried, but in vain, to drag him out. An unmethodical effort, aid awkwardly given, a wrong shake, might kill him. It was impossible to disengage him otherwise than by lifting the vehicle off of him. Javert, who had come up at the moment of the accident, had sent for a jack-screw.

M. Madeleine arrived. People stood aside respectfully.

'Help!' cried old Fauchelevent. 'Who will be good and save the old man?'

M. Madeleine turned towards those present:—

'Is there a jack-screw to be had?'

'One has been sent for,' answered the peasant.

'How long will it take to get it?'

'They have gone for the nearest, to Flachot's place, where there is a farrier; but it makes no difference; it will take a good quarter of an hour.'

'A quarter of an hour!' exclaimed Madeleine.

It had rained on the preceding night; the soil was soaked.

The cart was sinking deeper into the earth every moment, and crushing the old carter's breast more and more. It was evident that his ribs would be broken in five minutes more.

'It is impossible to wait another quarter of an hour,' said Madeleine to the peasants, who were staring at him.

'We must!'

'But it will be too late then! Don't you see that the cart is sinking?'

'Well!'

'Listen,' resumed Madeleine; 'there is still room enough under the cart to allow a man to crawl beneath it and raise it with his back. Only half a minute, and the poor man can be taken out. Is there any one here who has stout loins and heart? There are five louis d'or to be earned!'

Not a man in the group stirred.

'Ten louis,' said Madeleine.

The persons present dropped their eyes. One of them muttered: 'A man would need to be devilish strong. And then he runs the risk of getting crushed!'

'Come,' began Madeleine again, 'twenty louis.'

The same silence.

'It is not the will which is lacking,' said a voice.

M. Madeleine turned round, and recognized Javert. He had not noticed him on his arrival. Javert went on:—

'It is strength. One would have to be a terrible man to do such a thing as lift a cart like that on his back.'

Then, gazing fixedly at M. Madeleine, he went on, emphasizing every word that he uttered:—

'Monsieur Madeleine, I have never known but one man capable of doing what you ask.'

Madeleine shuddered.

Javert added, with an air of indifference, but without removing his eyes from Madeleine:—

'He was a convict.'

'Ah!' said Madeleine.

'In the galleys at Toulon.'

Madeleine turned pale.

Meanwhile, the cart continued to sink slowly. Father Fauchelevent rattled in the throat, and shrieked:—

'I am strangling! My ribs are breaking! a screw! something! Ah!'

Madeleine glanced about him.

'Is there, then, no one who wishes to earn twenty louis and save the life of this poor old man?'

No one stirred. Javert resumed:—

'I have never known but one man who could take the place of a screw, and he was that convict.'

'Ah! It is crushing me!' cried the old man.

Madeleine raised his head, met Javert's falcon eye still fixed upon him, looked at the motionless peasants, and smiled sadly. Then, without saying a word, he fell on his knees, and before the crowd had even had time to utter a cry, he was underneath the vehicle. A terrible moment of expectation and silence ensued.

They beheld Madeleine, almost flat on his stomach beneath

that terrible weight, make two vain efforts to bring his knees and his elbows together. They shouted to him, 'Father Madeleine, come out!' Old Fauchelevent himself said to him, 'Monsieur Madeleine, go away! You see that I am fated to die! Leave me! You will get yourself crushed also!' Madeleine made no reply.

All the spectators were panting. The wheels had continued to sink, and it had become almost impossible for Madeleine to make his way from under the vehicle.

Suddenly the enormous mass was seen to quiver, the cart rose slowly, the wheels half emerged from the ruts. They heard a stifled voice crying, 'Make haste! Help!' It was Madeleine, who had just made a final effort.

They rushed forwards. The devotion of a single man had given force and courage to all. The cart was raised by twenty arms. Old Fauchelevent was saved.

Madeleine rose. He was pale, though dripping with perspiration. His clothes were torn and covered with mud. All wept. The old man kissed his knees and called him the good God. As for him, he bore upon his countenance an indescribable expression of happy and celestial suffering, and he fixed his tranquil eye on Javert, who was still staring at him.

NEW THOUGHTS

ENOUGH ALREADY

Enid Stubin

We're not happy here in the States these days, but Thanksgiving came round as it does just when student portfolios are due and the penultimate drafts of essays have to be graded. My guests were due at 5:00, and this year I found myself at noon in a curious state of calm, or maybe it was just blank desertion: the turkey was in the oven, the side dishes ready, the usual cataract of paperwork contained in discreet shopping bags along the perimeter of my flat. The day before, hunting through a carton of sweet potatoes at the supermarket, I'd noticed a young woman reaching over me to heft a waxed yellow turnip, and I remembered an earlier Thanksgiving that had me following a recipe for Julia Child's Glazed Turnips—'It took me an hour just to whack the rind off one', I confessed aloud, then saw that the young woman had maybe a dozen in her basket. 'What will you do with all those?' I asked, astonished. 'I boil and then mash them—I grew up with them'. The pleasure in her voice impressed and heartened me. 'I've been to six markets and couldn't find any. I'm so happy to find these!' 'Those are some lucky people at your table', I told her.

That Glazed Turnip Thanksgiving, back in the eighties, was one of my early gatherings for orphans and the disaffected, people entirely lacking the animus and ancient grudges of family. Late in the morning a call came in from John as I was working on the mushroom-and-onion dressing. A speaker invited to New York University's Biography Seminar, Robert Browning's great-niece, was to have stayed with a couple on the Upper West Side, but they'd been called away for some family emergency and she was alone in the city over a holiday weekend. Could he bring her to Thanksgiving? But of course—there was an extra chair and more than enough to eat and drink. And when the lady arrived, decidedly glamorous but wet and chilled from the day's rainstorm, I scrabbled around in a closet and unearthed a facetious gift from Diana, something she'd found years earlier at the Women's Exchange, a bizarre if genteel crafts shop specializing in handmade Episcopalian aesthetics and ditzy luxury: a pair of house slippers in gold velvet, trimmed with gray fur and lined in shearling. Too big and too objectionable for me, they were just the thing for my guest, who shucked off her sodden shoes and accepted them happily along with a tumbler of Jameson's on ice. She'd been a vice-squad cop in Manchester, and my friend Dan had just been appointed chair of the New York State Assembly Committee on Corrections. I sat them next to each other and spent the rest of the meal in a haze of happiness, reveling in the gratifications of the host and the serendipity that had brought this stranger to my door. What a storyteller she was! We sat spellbound at her tales of guilt, retribution and the politics of a metropolitan police force years before anyone had even imagined Helen Mirren as Jane Tennison.

So this year, in the peculiar lull of that quiet moment, instead of the usual frenetic chaos of my kitchen prep, I sat down at the computer to type a message to John, who'd brought Robert Browning's great-niece to my table, along with a twelve-inch antique cast-iron skillet that had belonged to his mother. I was about to roast some new potatoes in it with olive oil and salt, I wrote, and nothing I cooked in that skillet ever came out less than spectacular. I reminded him of that long-ago visitor who'd captivated us and thanked him. And I reminded myself that along with the pressures and pieties of the season, we're brought back to the first Thanksgiving, a seventeenth-century feast framed poignantly by years of failure, hunger and privation, when finally, as William Bradford wrote in *Of Plymouth Plantation*, 'All had their hungrie bellies filled'. In that context, the meal is sacrament rather than neurotic excess, and the occasion offers hope in the wake of despair. And the guests—the guests provide the grace.

So let's be hopeful, my dears. Me, I'm doing my best. Every December I schedule an appointment with Dr Long for a skin cancer check, an examination at which I attempt to divert at least one of us with my tales of the literary world. This year I went to the Norman Mailer Society conference in Sarasota, Florida, where I made friends with a Russian scholar who saw affinities between Mailer and Isaac Babel. I had a neat little Pushkin Press edition of *Odessa Stories*, with a racy new translation by Boris Dralyuk, for Dr Long. But he was ready for me with his own account of having read *A Moveable Feast* and marveled at the ill will on display—'So mean, so petty, so vicious'—for Fitzgerald. Yes, I agreed, you really had to go to Hemingway for that level of cruelty. But then I began a piece on Mailer by apologizing for a nasty crack I'd made and been called on back in 2008. At the Sarasota conference a media expert and producer showed excerpts from TV interviews; in one with Dick Cavett, Mailer was clearly out of sorts and control, and Cavett and his other guests, Gore Vidal and Janet Flanner, ganged up on him. How wounded Mailer, that self-styled street brawler and professional tough guy, could be! I mentioned the hurt registered on his face for long televised close-ups to his daughter Susan, an analyst, as we left the session. 'No one ever comments on that', she told me quietly.

From the pleasures and pains of scholarly spite we moved to a consideration of the new Edward Garnett biography by Helen Smith and the thin-skinned narcissism of our president. The daily outrages and staggering ineptitude have gotten to me, I'm afraid, and I went into my default mode of hand-wringing. Given the coarsening of our political rhetoric, the pathology on parade, how could we endure another three years of this huckster? But Dr Long was resolute, anticipating a watershed moment like the one at the 1954 Army-McCarthy hearings at which Joseph Welch, a Boston lawyer hired to represent the United States Army, faced down Senator Joseph McCarthy. McCarthy and his chief counsel

Roy Cohn had accused one of Welch's young attorneys of having connections to a Communist organization. Furious, Welch said, 'Until this moment, Senator, I think I never really gauged your cruelty or your recklessness'. When McCarthy tried to continue, Welch interrupted him: 'Let us not assassinate this lad further, Senator. You have done enough. Have you no sense of decency, sir, at long last? Have you left no sense of decency?' Within weeks McCarthy was abandoned by his cronies; Welch's indignation had struck a nerve in the American consciousness. Dr Long's delivery, timed to coincide with his exit, cheered me no end. When all that's spoke is marr'd, the words we have left—of outrage, of appreciation, of gratitude—assume the weight of justice.

BUCK'S QUIZ

STORMY WEATHER

Angela Macmillan

1. In which 2009 novel is a climatologist forced to take up the life of a down and out?

2. 'I should have kissed her if the rain / Had lasted a minute more.' Who is the poet?

3. A thunderstorm brings to an end not only a stifling hot Edwardian summer but also a childhood innocence, in which novel?

4. Which poem opens on a scene after a night storm: 'But now the sun is rising calm and bright; / The birds are singing in the distant woods'?

5. The phrase, 'It was a dark and stormy night' has become an archetypal example of purple prose but who was the original author?

6. Who exhorts the storm: 'And thou, all-shaking thunder, /Smite flat the thick rotundity o' the world! /Crack nature's moulds, an germens spill at once,/That make ingrateful man!'?

7. Captain MacWhirr steers the SS Nan-Shan through a Pacific storm in which novel?

8. 'My mother, who hates thunder storms, /Holds up each summer day and shakes /It out suspiciously, lest swarms /Of grape-dark clouds are lurking there'. Whose mother is this?

9. The great storm of 1987 is key in an important scene at the end of which Booker Prize winning novel?

10. 'Shantih shantih shantih' are the last words of the final section of a long poem. What is this section called?

ACROSS

* **1 and 19 down.** 26's version of what he learnt about the north (3, 3, 7)

4. Discovers copies and reacts badly (6)

9. Cause of decreased perception in Rees Mogg's outlook (4)

10. Places to improve coarse materials, free rein is exercised here (10)

*__11.__ See 26 across

12. Those requiring the most assistance starting in North East ending down in East Surrey town (8)

13. After this it's at your own risk but see day out (3-2, 4)

*__15, 18 down and 16 across.__ Journey into the unknown for 26's second collection (4, 4, 3, 4)

*__16.__ See 15 across

17. Medically sensitive and easily annoyed (9)

21. Visible dance when one transferring to another? (4, 4)

22. Usually more than one of these and can be good news at Christmas (6)

24. Transparent class of receiver? (7, 3)

25. Final word lies in fundamental principles (4)

*__26 and 11 across.__ Sadly his 'squat pen' now rests in peace (6, 6)

27. Undistinguished partner of a vain strutting fellow (6)

DOWN

1. Moderates tantrums (7)

2. British Museum collection sends Nigel spinning! (5)

3. A dreary miscellany but impressively displayed (7)

5. Church musician when late sees double (6)

6. Turn over Marconi account for sign of something amiss (9)

7. Inventor of his own poetic form for his own form of royalty (7)

*__8.__ See 23 down

14. Bring ease transforming region where east meets west (6, 3)

16. Conducts oneself inside Port Sunlight's environs (7)

18. See 15 across

*__19.__ See 1 across

20. In Paris we have seen it all before (4, 2)

23 and 8 down. Curtains for Charles Darwin maybe? (5, 2, 1, 10)

*Clues with an asterisk have a common theme

PRIZES

The winner of the Crossword (plucked in time-honoured tradition from a hat) will receive a book prize courtesy of Vintage Classics, and the same to the winner of the fiendishly difficult Buck's Quiz.

Congratulations to R.Reynolds and to Lois Zellas who win the Cassandra Crossword prize, and to Joyce Allen who beat Buck's Quiz.

Please send your solutions (marked Cassandra Crossword or Buck's Quiz) to The Reader, Calderstones Mansion House, Calderstones Park, Liverpool, L18 3JB. The deadline for answers is 25 February 2018.

ANSWERS

CASSANDRA CROSSWORD NO. 59

Across

1. Eradicate 10. Delft 11. Anita 12. Olive Tree 13. Day Lily 14. Friends 17. Libra 19. And 20. Putti 21. Cholera 22. Leaving 24. Baksheesh 26. Hotel 28. Cream 29. Tarantino

Down

1. Hera 2. Family 3. Dilapidate 4. Jalopy 5. Seriffed 6. Idle 7. Clarinet 8. At me 13. Du lac 15. Impeaching 16. Swing 18. Brookner 19. Analects 22. Lahore 23. Intuit 24. Back 25. Home 27. Look

BUCK'S QUIZ NO. 67

1. Marlin 2. Trout 3. A pike 4. 'Silver', Walter de la Mare 5. Lorna Doone 6. *A River Runs Through It*, Norman Maclean 7. *Moby Dick* 8. *The Compleat Angler*, Izaak Walton 9. Jeremy Fisher 10. 'How to Get On in Society', John Betjeman

CONTRIBUTORS

Michael Balogun Actor, 33. He grew up in South London and spent much of his younger life in and out of prison. Graduated from RADA after three years training. Played Shaun in the nationwide tour of Duncan Macmillan's *People, Places and Things*. He will shortly take up his first TV role.

Elizabeth Bonapace is in her final year of an MA in Shakespeare & Education at the Shakespeare Institute. She is currently involved in research to create a Shakespearean-themed, vocabulary-building workshop for primary aged children, particularly those on the autistic spectrum.

Frank Cottrell Boyce is an award-winning novelist and screen writer. Books include *Millions, Framed, Cosmic,* and the sequels to Ian Fleming's *Chitty Chitty Bang Bang*. His most recent book is *The Astounding Broccoli Boy* (2016). He was the writer for the 2012 London Summer Olympics Opening Ceremony.

Iain Britton Since 2008, he has had five collections of poems published, mainly in the UK. Recently, poems have been published or are forthcoming in magazines including *Cordite*, the *Harvard Review*, *POETRY*, *STAND*, *Poetry Wales*, *AGENDA*, and many others. A new collection *THE INTAGLIO POEMS* was published by Hesterglock Press, 2017.

Grace (Farrington) Frame has worked with The Reader since 2009 and is currently a Learning and Quality Leader.

John Levett has published many collections of poetry, his latest, *A Song About You,* being published by Shoestring Press in December 2017. He is a winner of the National Poetry Competition and the *New Statesman*'s Prudence Farmer Award.

Andrew McMillan was born in South Yorkshire in 1988; his debut collection *physical* was the first ever poetry collection to win The Guardian First Book Award. His second collection, *playtime*, will be published by Jonathan Cape in 2018. He is senior lecturer at the Manchester Writing School at MMU and lives in Manchester.

Ian McMillan was born in 1956 and has been a freelance writer/performer /broadcaster since 1981. He presents *The Verb* on BBC Radio 3 every Friday night.

Richard Meier won the Picador Poetry Prize in 2010, as a result of which his first collection, *Misadventure*, was published in 2012. His second collection is due from Picador later this year.

Craig Parkinson Actor, 41. He grew up in Blackpool and went to drama school in London. Known for TV roles in E4's *Misfits* and in BBC's *Line of Duty*, he has also appeared in several independent films. Craig (with producer Thomas Griffin) recently created Two Shot Podcast – a podcast about acting. Lives in the Cotswolds with his wife – actor Susan Lynch – and son.

Wilbur Sanders (1936–2002) Born and raised in New Zealand. He became lecturer and fellow of Selwyn College, Cambridge, retiring 2001. Books include *The Dramatist and the Received Idea* (1968), *John Donne's Poetry* (1971) and two novels, *Like the Big Wolves* (1985) and *Hector's Folly* (1995).

David Shackleton is a Lecturer in English at the University of Exeter. He has published articles in *The Review of English Studies* and *Victorian Literature and Culture*, and interviews regularly for the book-recommendation website Five Books.

Enid Stubin is Associate Professor of English at Kingsborough Community College of the City University of New York and Adjunct Professor of Humanities at NY University's School of Continuing and Professional Studies.

Matthias Weaver lives in the north west of England, where he works in support of people with learning disabilities. His work has appeared in *Autumn Sky Poetry* and *Tortoise*, and he was a featured poet in the August 2017 episode of the Lunar Poetry podcast.

Distribution Information

Trade orders Contact Mark Chilver, Magazine Department, Central Books

email: mark@centralbooks.com
web: www.centralbooks.com
tel: 0845 458 9925   fax: 0845 458 9912
Central Books, 99 Wallis Road, London, E9 5LN

All other queries regarding trade orders or institutional subscriptions
Contact The Reader Office

email: magazine@thereader.org.uk
tel: 0151 729 2200

SUBSCRIBE

£18 per year with Direct Debit

Print off an order form from our website (www.thereader. org.uk), call us on 0151 729 2200 or email (magazine@ thereader.org.uk) and we will send you a form in the post.

Cost by Cheque or PayPal:

UK Subscription: four issues for £24 (inc. p&p)
Abroad Subscription: four issues for £36 (inc. p&p)

Please make cheques payable to The Reader and post to: The Reader, FREEPOST RSSL-UHCB-EKKE, Calderstones Mansion House, Calderstones Park, Liverpool, L18 3JB.

Don't forget to include your name and address, and the issue number with which you would like your subscription to begin.

The cheapest payment method for overseas readers is by PayPal via our website: www.thereader.org.uk

Please direct email enquiries to:
subscriptions@thereader.org.uk

the reader